Modern Critical Interpretations

John Webster's
The Duchess of Malfi

Modern Critical Interpretations

These and other titles in preparation

Modern Critical Interpretations

John Webster's
The Duchess of Malfi

Edited and with an introduction by

Harold Bloom
Sterling Professor of the Humanities
Yale University

Chelsea House Publishers ◇ *1987*
NEW YORK ◇ NEW HAVEN ◇ PHILADELPHIA

Library of Congress Cataloging-in-Publication Data
John Webster's The Duchess of Malfi.
    (Modern critical interpretations)
    Bibliography: p.
    Includes index.
    Summary: A collection of essays on Webster's tragic drama
"The Duchess of Malfi" arranged in chronological order of
publication.
    1. Webster, John, 1580?–1625? Duchess of Malfi.
[1. Webster, John, 1580?–1625? Duchess of Malfi. 2. English
literature—History and criticism] I. Bloom,
Harold.   II. Series.
PR3184.D83J64   1987   822'.3   87-9398
 ISBN 0-87754-920-6 (alk. paper)

Contents

Editor's Note

This book brings together a representative selection of what I judge to be the best modern criticism of John Webster's tragic drama *The Duchess of Malfi*. The critical essays are reprinted here in the chronological sequence of their original publication. I am grateful to Kathryn Treadwell for her assistance as a researcher upon this volume.

My introduction traces the fortunes of the Elizabethan-Jacobean hero-villain, from Marlowe through Shakespeare on to Marston and Tourneur, to culminate in Webster's superb Bosola in *The Duchess of Malfi*.

Michael R. Best begins the chronological sequence with a study of the precariously balanced structure of the *Duchess*, while Leslie Duer illuminates the eccentric visionary landscapes of the play.

The distinguished Elizabethan scholar Muriel Bradbrook sets the cultural contexts for the *Duchess*, after which Bettie Anne Doebler gives the background for the theology of dying in Webster's drama.

Jacqueline Pearson argues that the final act of the *Duchess* is anti-tragedy, while John L. Selzer studies the Renaissance idea of degree against merit that informs the play's marriage plot.

In a fine essay on the historical contexts of Websterian theater, Catherine Belsey helps us to grasp the drama's antithetical elements. Lisa Jardine completes this book with an examination of Renaissance inheritance practices so as to define the Duchess's real as against her presumptive power, uncertain because of her equivocal status as a woman.

Introduction

> Why, I, in this weak piping time of peace,
> Have no delight to pass away the time,
> Unless to see my shadow in the sun
> And descant on mine own deformity.
> And therefore, since I cannot prove a lover
> To entertain these fair well-spoken days,
> I am determined to prove a villain
> And hate the idle pleasures of these days.
>
> (1.1.24–31)

The opening ferocity of Richard, still Duke of Gloucester, in *The Tragedy of Richard the Third,* is hardly more than a fresh starting-point for the development of the Elizabethan and Jacobean hero-villain after Marlowe, and yet it seems to transform Tamburlaine and Barabas utterly. Richard's peculiarly self-conscious pleasure in his own audacity is crossed by the sense of what it means to see one's own deformed shadow in the sun. We are closer already not only to Edmund and Iago than to Barabas, but especially closer to Webster's Lodovico who so sublimely says: "I limn'd this night-piece and it was my best." Except for Iago, nothing seems farther advanced in this desperate mode than Webster's Bosola:

> O direful misprision!
> I will not imitate things glorious
> No more than base: I'll be mine own example.—
> On, on, and look thou represent, for silence,
> The thing thou bear'st.
>
> (5.4.87–91)

Iago is beyond even this denial of representation, because he does will silence:

1

> Demand me nothing; what you know, you know;
> From this time forth I never will speak word.
>
> (5.2.303–4)

Iago is no hero-villain, and no shift of perspective will make him into one. Pragmatically, the authentic hero-villain in Shakespeare might be judged to be Hamlet, but no audience would agree. Macbeth could justify the description, except that the cosmos of his drama is too estranged from any normative representation for the term hero-villain to have its oxymoronic coherence. Richard and Edmund would appear to be the models, beyond Marlowe, that could have inspired Webster and his fellows, but Edmund is too uncanny and superb a representation to provoke emulation. That returns us to Richard:

> Was ever woman in this humor woo'd?
> Was ever woman in this humor won?
> I'll have her, but I will not keep her long.
> What? I, that kill'd her husband and his father,
> To take her in her heart's extremest hate,
> With curses in her mouth, tears in her eyes,
> The bleeding witness of my hatred by,
> Having God, her conscience, and these bars against me,
> And I no friends to back my suit [at all]
> But the plain devil and dissembling looks?
> And yet to win her! All the world to nothing!
> Hah!
> Hath she forgot already that brave prince,
> Edward, her lord, whom I, some three months since,
> Stabb'd in my angry mood at Tewksbury?
> A sweeter and a lovelier gentleman,
> Fram'd in the prodigality of nature—
> Young, valiant, wise, and (no doubt) right royal—
> The spacious world cannot again afford.
> And will she yet abase her eyes on me,
> That cropp'd the golden prime of this sweet prince
> And made her widow to a woeful bed?
> On me, whose all not equals Edward's moi'ty?
> On me, that halts and am misshapen thus?
> My dukedom to a beggarly denier,
> I do mistake my person all this while!
> Upon my life, she finds (although I cannot)

> Myself to be a marv'llous proper man.
> I'll be at charges for a looking-glass,
> And entertain a score or two of tailors
> To study fashions to adorn my body:
> Since I am crept in favor with myself,
> I will maintain it with some little cost.
> But first I'll turn yon fellow in his grave,
> And then return lamenting to my love.
> Shine out, fair sun, till I have bought a glass,
> That I may see my shadow as I pass.
>
> (1.2.227–63)

Richard's only earlier delight was "to see my shadow in the sun /And descant on mine own deformity." His savage delight in the success of his own manipulative rhetoric now transforms his earlier trope into the exultant command: "Shine out, fair sun, till I have bought a glass, / That I may see my shadow as I pass." That transformation is the formula for interpreting the Jacobean hero-villain and his varied progeny: Milton's Satan, the Poet in Shelley's *Alastor,* Wordsworth's Oswald in *The Borderers,* Byron's Manfred and Cain, Browning's Childe Roland, Tennyson's Ulysses, Melville's Captain Ahab, Hawthorne's Chillingworth, down to Nathanael West's Shrike in *Miss Lonelyhearts,* who perhaps ends the tradition. The manipulative, highly self-conscious, obsessed hero-villain, whether Machiavellian plotter or later, idealistic quester, ruined or not, moves himself from being the passive sufferer of his own moral and/or physical deformity to becoming a highly active melodramatist. Instead of standing in the light of nature to observe his own shadow, and then have to take his own deformity as subject, he rather commands nature to throw its light upon his own glass of representation, so that his own shadow will be visible only for an instant as he passes on to the triumph of his will over others.

II

No figure in this tradition delights me personally more than Barabas, Marlowe's Jew of Malta, who so fittingly is introduced by Machiavel himself:

> Albeit the world think Machevill is dead,
> Yet was his soul but flown beyond the Alps,
> And now the Guise is dead, is come from France
> To view this land, and frolic with his friends.

To some perhaps my name is odious,
But such as love me, guard me from their tongues,
And let them know that I am Machevill,
And weigh not men, and therefore not men's words.
Admired I am of those that hate me most.
Though some speak openly against my books,
Yet will they read me, and thereby attain
To Peter's chair: and when they cast me off,
Are poisoned by my climbing followers.
I count religion but a childish toy,
And hold there is no sin but ignorance.
Birds of the air will tell of murders past?
I am ashamed to hear such fooleries.
Many will talk of title to a crown.
What right had Caesar to the empery?
Might first made kings, and laws were then most sure
When like the Draco's they were writ in blood.
Hence comes it, that a strong built citadel
Commands much more than letters can import:
Which maxima had Phalaris observed,
H'had never bellowed in a brazen bull
Of great ones' envy; o' th' poor petty wits,
Let me be envied and not pitièd!
But whither am I bound, I come not, I,
To read a lecture here in Britanie,
But to present the tragedy of a Jew,
Who smiles to see how full his bags are crammed,
Which money was not got without my means.
I crave but this, grace him as he deserves,
And let him not be entertained the worse
Because he favours me.

(Prologue)

From Shakespeare's Richard III and Macbeth through Webster's Bosola and Flamineo on to Melville's Ahab and, finally, to West's Shrike, the descendants of Marlowe's Machiavel have held there is no sin but ignorance, and have become involuntary parodies of what ancient heresy called *gnosis,* a knowing in which the knower seeks the knowledge of the abyss. Nihilism, uncanny even to Nietzsche, is the atmosphere breathed cannily by the Jacobean hero-villain, who invariably domesticates the abyss. Barabas,

Machiavel's favorite, wins our zestful regard because of the Groucho Marxian vitalism of his deliciously evil self-knowings:

> As for myself, I walk abroad a-nights,
> And kill sick people groaning under walls:
> Sometimes I go about and poison wells;
> And now and then, to cherish Christian thieves,
> I am content to lose some of my crowns;
> That I may, walking in my gallery,
> See 'em go pinioned along by my door.
> Being young I studied physic, and began
> To practise first upon the Italian;
> There I enriched the priests with burials,
> And always kept the sexton's arms in ure
> With digging graves and ringing dead men's knells:
> And after that was I an engineer,
> And in the wars 'twixt France and Germany,
> Under pretence of helping Charles the Fifth,
> Slew friend and enemy with my stratagems.
> Then after that was I an usurer,
> And with extorting, cozening, forfeiting,
> And tricks belonging unto brokery,
> I filled the jails with bankrouts in a year,
> And with young orphans planted hospitals,
> And every moon made some or other mad,
> And now and then one hang himself for grief,
> Pinning upon his breast a long great scroll
> How I with interest tormented him.
> But mark how I am blest for plaguing them,
> I have as much coin as will buy the town.
> But tell me now, how hast thou spent thy time?
>   (2.3.178–205)

The hyperboles here are so outrageous that Marlowe's insouciant identification with Barabas becomes palpable, and we begin to feel that this is how Tamburlaine the Great would sound and act if he had to adjust his overreachings to the limits of being a Jew in Christian Malta. Barabas is too splendidly grotesque a mockery to set a pattern for dramatic poets like Webster, Tourneur, Ford, and Middleton. They found their model for revenge tragedy in Kyd rather than Shakespeare, for many of the same reasons that they based their dark knowers upon Marston's Malevole in

The Malcontent rather than upon Barabas. We begin to hear in Malevole what will culminate in Tourneur's *The Revenger's Tragedy* and in Webster's *The White Devil* and *The Duchess of Malfi*. Disdaining to take revenge upon his craven enemy, Mendoza, Malevole expresses a contempt so intense and so universal as to open up the abyss of nihilism:

> O, I have seen strange accidents of state!
> The flatterer, like the ivy, clip the oak,
> And waste it to the heart; lust so confirm'd,
> That the black act of sin itself not sham'd
> To be term'd courtship.
> O, they that are as great as be their sins,
> Let them remember that th' inconstant people
> Love many princes merely for their faces
> And outward shows; and they do covet more
> To have a sight of these than of their virtues.
> Yet thus much let the great ones still conceive,
> When they observe not heaven's impos'd conditions,
> They are no kings, but forfeit their commissions.
> (scene 5, ll. 152–64)

That, for a Jacobean, leaves not much, and is the prelude to the hysterical eloquence of Tourneur's Vindice the revenger:

> And now methinks I could e'en chide myself
> For doting on her beauty, though her death
> Shall be revenged after no common action.
> Does the silkworm expand her yellow labors
> For thee? For thee does she undo herself?
> Are lordships sold to maintain ladyships
> For the poor benefit of a bewitching minute?
> Why does yon fellow falsify highways
> And put his life between the judge's lips
> To refine such a thing, keeps horse and men
> To beat their valors for her?
> Surely we're all mad people and they,
> Whom we think are, are not: we mistake those.
> 'Tis we are mad in sense, they but in clothes.
>
> . . . .
>
> Does every proud and self-affecting dame
> Camphor her face for this, and grieve her maker

In sinful baths of milk, when many an infant starves
For her superfluous outside—all for this?
Who now bids twenty pound a night, prepares
Music, perfumes and sweetmeats? All are hushed,
Thou may'st lie chaste now! It were fine, methinks,
To have thee seen at revels, forgetful feasts
And unclean brothels; sure 'twould fright the sinner
And make him a good coward, put a reveler
Out of his antic amble,
And cloy an epicure with empty dishes.
Here might a scornful and ambitious woman
Look through and through herself; see, ladies, with false
    forms
You deceive men but cannot deceive worms.
Now to my tragic business. Look you, brother,
I have not fashioned this only for show
And useless property, no—it shall bear a part
E'en in it own revenge. This very skull,
Whose mistress the duke poisoned with this drug,
The mortal curse of the earth, shall be revenged
In the like strain and kiss his lips to death.
As much as the dumb thing can, he shall feel;
What fails in poison we'll supply in steel.

                                 (3.5.68–106)

It takes some considerable effort to recall that Vindice is addressing the skull of his martyred mistress, and that he considers her, or any woman whatsoever, worth revenging. These remarkable lines were much admired by T. S. Eliot, and one sees why; they are close to his ideal for dramatic poetry, and their intense aversion to female sexuality suited his own difficult marital circumstances during one bad phase of his life. What the passage clearly evidences is that Vindice is a true Jacobean hero-villain; he is more than skeptical as to the value of his own motivations, or of anyone else's as well. But this is hardly the historical skepticism that scholars delight in tracing; it has little to do with the pragmatism of Machiavelli, the naturalism of Montaigne, or the Hermeticism of Bruno. The horror of nature involved, whatever Tourneur's personal pathology, amounts to a kind of Gnostic asceticism, akin to the difficult stance of Macbeth and Lady Macbeth. Perhaps the hero-villain, like Milton's Satan, is truly in rebellion against the God of the Jews and the Christians, the God of this world.

III

Though the central tradition of the hero-villain goes directly from Shakespeare through Milton on to the High Romantics and their heirs, we might be puzzled at certain strains in Browning, Tennyson, Hawthorne, and Melville, if we had not read John Webster's two astonishing plays, *The White Devil* and *The Duchess of Malfi*. Russell Fraser memorably caught Webster's curious link to Marlowe, whom he otherwise scarcely resembles:

> His violent protagonists are memorable as they are endowed with the same amoral energy with which Barabas and Tamburlaine and Mortimer are endowed. Unlike these Marlovian heroes or hero-villains, they do not speak to us—quoting from Michael Drayton's tribute to Marlowe—of "brave translunary things," rather of the charnel house and the grisly business appurtenant to it.

Here is the death scene of Flamineo, and of his sister, Vittoria Corombona, in *The White Devil*:

> VITTORIA COROMBONA. Oh, my greatest sin lay in my
>   blood!
> Now my blood pays for't.
> FLAMINEO.   Thou'rt a noble sister!
> I love thee now. If woman do breed man,
> She ought to teach him manhood. Fare thee well.
> Know, many glorious women that are famed
> For masculine virtue have been vicious,
> Only a happier silence did betide them.
> She hath no faults who hath the art to hide them.
> VITTORIA COROMBONA. My soul, like to a ship in a black
>   storm,
> Is driven I know not whither.
> FLAMINEO.   Then cast anchor.
> Prosperity doth bewitch men, seeming clear,
> But seas do laugh, show white, when rocks are near.
> We cease to grieve, cease to be fortune's slaves,
> Nay, cease to die, by dying. Art thou gone?
> And thou so near the bottom? False report,
> Which says that women vie with the nine Muses
> For nine tough durable lives! I do not look
> Who went before, nor who shall follow me;

No, at myself I will begin and end.
While we look up to heaven, we confound
Knowledge with knowledge. Oh, I am in a mist!
VITTORIA COROMBONA. Oh, happy they that never saw the
    court,
Nor ever knew great men but by report!
                  VITTORIA dies.
FLAMINEO. I recover like a spent taper, for a flash,
    And instantly go out.
      Let all that belong to great men remember the
      old wives' tradition, to be like the lions i' the
      Tower on Candlemas-day: to mourn if the sun
      shine, for fear of the pitiful remainder of
      winter to come.
'Tis well yet there's some goodness in my death;
My life was a black charnel. I have caught
An everlasting cold; I have lost my voice
Most irrecoverably. Farewell, glorious villains!
This busy trade of life appears most vain,
Since rest breeds rest where all seek pain by pain.
Let no harsh flattering bells resound my knell;
Strike, thunder, and strike loud, to my farewell!
                       Dies.
                (5.6.241–77)

Vittoria Corombona rides her black ship to Hell without final knowledge, but Flamineo is a knower, a Machiavel in the high Marlovian sense, which has its Gnostic aspect. By beginning and ending "at myself," Flamineo seeks to avoid a final agon between his self-knowledge and a rival Christian knowledge: "While we look up to heaven, we confound / Knowledge with knowledge." And yet, Flamineo cries out: "Oh, I am in a mist!", which is what it is to the confounded, and perhaps leads to the self-epitaph: "My life was a black charnel." The mist appears also in the death speech of a greater hero-villain than Flamineo, Bosola in *The Duchess of Malfi*:

    In a mist; I know not how;
    Such a mistake as I have often seen
    In a play. Oh, I am gone.
    We are only like dead walls, or vaulted graves
    That ruined, yields no echo. Fare you well;
    It may be pain, but no harm to me to die

> In so good a quarrel. Oh, this gloomy world,
> In what a shadow, or deep pit of darkness
> Doth womanish and fearful mankind live?
> Let worthy minds ne'er stagger in distrust
> To suffer death or shame for what is just.
> Mine is another voyage.
>
> *Dies.*
> (5.5.94–105)

Bosola's final vision is of the cosmic emptiness, what the Gnostics called the *kenoma*, into which we have been thrown: "a shadow, or deep pit of darkness." When Bosola dies, saying, "Mine is another voyage," he may mean simply that he is not suffering death for what is just, unlike those who have "worthy minds." But this is Bosola, master of direful misprision, whose motto is: "I will not imitate things glorious, / No more than base; I'll be mine own example." This repudiation of any just representation of essential nature is also a Gnostic repudiation of nature, in favor of an antithetical quest: "On, on, and look thou represent, for silence, / The thing thou bear'st." What Bosola both carries and endures, and so represents, by a kind of super-mimesis, is that dark quest, whose admonition, "on, on" summons one to the final phrase: "Mine is another voyage." As antithetical quester, Bosola prophesies Milton's Satan voyaging through Chaos toward the New World of Eden, and all those destructive intensities of wandering self-consciousness from Wordsworth's Solitary through the Poet of *Alastor* on to their culmination in the hero-villain who recites the great dramatic monologue "Childe Roland to the Dark Tower Came":

> Burningly it came on me all at once,
>   This was the place! those two hills on the right,
>   Crouched like two bulls locked horn in horn in fight;
> While to the left, a tall scalped mountain . . . Dunce,
> Dotard, a-dozing at the very nonce,
>   After a life spent training for the sight!
>
> What in the midst lay but the Tower itself?
>   The round squat turret, blind as the fool's heart,
>   Built of brown stone, without a counterpart
> In the whole world. The tempest's mocking elf
> Points to the shipman thus the unseen shelf
>   He strikes on, only when the timbers start.

> Not see? because of night perhaps?—why, day
>> Came back again for that! before it left,
>> The dying sunset kindled through a cleft:
> The hills, like giants at a hunting, lay,
> Chin upon hand, to see the game at bay,—
>> "Now stab and end the creature—to the heft!"
>>> (ll. 175–92)

The Machiavel spends a life training for the sight, and yet is self-betrayed, because he is self-condemned to be "blind as the fool's heart." He will see, at the last, and he will know, and yet all that he will see and know are the lost adventurers his peers, who, like him, have come upon the Dark Tower unaware. The Jacobean hero-villain, at the end, touches the limit of manipulative self-knowledge, and in touching that limit gives birth to the High Romantic self-consciousness which we cannot evade, and which remains the affliction of our post-Modernism, so-called, as it was of every Modernism, from Milton to our present moment.

A Precarious Balance: Structure in *The Duchess of Malfi*

Michael R. Best

Shakespeare's Ulysses, eloquent enunciator of the great Elizabethan commonplaces of degree and order, has some comments on the nature of discord which sound remarkably like a description of the two brothers of the Duchess of Malfi. When degree is removed,

> everything includes itself in power,
> Power into will, will into appetite;
> And appetite, an universal wolf,
> So doubly seconded with will and power,
> Must make perforce an universal prey,
> And last eat up himself.
> (*Troilus and Cressida*, 1.3.119–24)

In Webster's play, the Cardinal is concerned with power and will, Ferdinand with will and appetite. J. R. Brown points out [in the Revels edition] that of the two brothers, one "seems wholly ruled by his intelligence; the other directly contrasted to him by giving way to his passions." The distinction can be seen in terms of the concepts which Ulysses is using, for he is describing the chaos which ensues when the baser passions of the body control man's reason; the relationship between the body and the mind of man was traditionally explained by an interdependence between the sensitive soul, which was the seat of the senses and passions, and the rational soul,

From *Shakespeare and Some Others: Essays on Shakespeare and Some of his Contemporaries*, edited by Alan Brissenden. © 1976 by Michael R. Best. University of Adelaide, Department of English, 1976.

which distinguished man from beast and controlled the understanding and the will, or power of choice. The brothers are governed by will uncontrolled by any other higher impulse of conscience or right reason; the Cardinal chooses to seek power through the use of his understanding, or intelligence, and Ferdinand, to whom Ulysses' image of the wolf is obviously appropriate, becomes progressively more obsessed by his emotions and senses.

Ferdinand is shown throughout the play as a man of passionate physical action. He is introduced as he leaves the field of "sportiue-action," hankering after "action indeed," and his presence on stage is almost always associated with violence. Even a rare moment of quietness is described by Antonio in terms of suppressed anger: "Those houses, that are haunted, are most still, / Till the diuell be vp" (all quotations from the play are from the 1623 quarto). The prevailing images connected with Ferdinand are those of animals, most obviously the wolf, transferred to the Duchess's "Cubbs" or "young Wolffes," and becoming more literal than metaphorical in the lycanthropia of the last act, where Ferdinand is probably trying to reveal his own crime by stealing forth "to Church-yards in the dead of night, / [To] dig dead bodies vp," since he had earlier prophesied to Bosola, after the murder of the Duchess, that

> The Wolfe shall find her Graue, and scrape it vp:
> Not to deuoure the corpes, but to discouer
> The horrid murther.

At the climax of the play, after calling for a fresh horse, Ferdinand, in his imagination, becomes the horse itself: "Giue me some wet hay, I am broken winded." The effect of such metaphor, made more powerful by the madness that sees it as reality, is to emphasize in Ferdinand the physical and the irrational—the beast in man. Further, Ferdinand perceives the relationship with his sister in sensuously physical terms, and it is with a painful intensity that he imagines the Duchess's sexual encounters:

> Happily, with some strong thigh'd Bargeman;
> Or one th' wood-yard, that can quoit the sledge,
> Or tosse the barre, or else some louely Squire
> That carries coles vp, to her priuy lodgings.

When Bosola refers in passing to her "delicate skin," Ferdinand's response is to damn "that body of hers" while, with an anticipation of madness, he speaks of his own blood running in her veins, and claims that this shared blood is "more worth / Then that which thou [Bosola] wouldst comfort, (call'd a soule)." Ferdinand not only rejects the soul as inferior to the body, but he speaks of the "most imperfect light of humaine reason" and seems to be at least partially aware of the irrationality of his motives:

> FERDINAND. I would not haue her marry againe.
> BOSOLA. No, Sir?
> FERDINAND. Doe not you aske the reason: but be satisfied, I
>   say I would not.

His later attempts to explain his actions as the result of the Duchess's disrespect for religion or the money he hoped to gain by her death are slender rationalizations, produced well after the depth and intensity of his passion have been established. The picture that emerges is of a character who, in terms of the traditional categories of human nature, rejects the spiritual and rational for the bestial life of the senses.

The character of the Cardinal is strongly contrasted, most obviously in the scene where the brothers hear the news of the birth of the Duchess's first child by Antonio. Throughout the scene the Cardinal retains his control, and, indeed, seems to become colder as Ferdinand becomes more violent. He attempts to moderate his brother's passion—"Speake lower . . . Why doe you make your selfe / So wild a Tempest?"—and criticizes Ferdinand's lack of rational balance:

> You flie beyond your reason.
>   . . . I can be angry
> Without this rupture, there is not in nature
> A thing, that makes man so deform'd, so beastly,
> As doth intemperate anger.

The Cardinal's own physical appetite is at all times under the control of his mind. Delio comments on his reputation as a man of action:

> They say he's a braue fellow,
> Will play his fiue thousand crownes, at Tennis, Daunce,
> Court Ladies, and one that hath fought single Combats

But Antonio's comment is more perceptive:

> Some such flashes superficially hang on him, for forme:
> But obserue his inward Character: he is a melancholly
> Church-man,

and he goes on to establish the Cardinal as the type of the machiavel:

> Where he is iealious of any man,
> He laies worse plots for them, then euer was impos'd on
> *Hercules:* for he strewes in his way Flatt[er]ers, Panders,
> Intelligencers, Atheists, and a thousand such politicall
> Monsters.

The tendency of the machiavel to overreach himself is shown to be a failing of the Cardinal, as Antonio goes on to tell of his too blatant bribery in attempting to become Pope. The accuracy of Antonio's character sketch is immediatlely proven when the Cardinal chooses Bosola as his spy, and manages not to "be seene in't" manipulating him at second hand through his brother. The Cardinal also keeps a mistress to minister to his physical needs, but the extent to which he controls his feelings for her demonstrates the extent of his control over himself. He praises her witty falsehood, appears unmoved by her physical beauty, and within a few lines of their dialogue (2.4) has manipulated her to tears. The superior manipulative skill of the Cardinal is shown later in the scene when Julia demonstrates that her wit, though no match for her lover's, is more than adequate to bemuse Delio. Later, of course, the Cardinal disposes of Julia in a manner sufficiently callous to suggest that he uses her simply to release his sexual urge rather than to indulge it. The Cardinal's devious mind is firmly in control of his senses, even if his physical desires are not wholly repressed, and in this respect he is the opposite of his brother. Like Ferdinand, however, the Cardinal rejects, or suppresses, conscience: "I would pray now: but the Diuell takes away my heart / For hauing any confidence in Praier" and later he finds a guilty conscience merely "tedious," though its effect is described in a justly famous image,

> When I looke into the Fish-ponds, in my Garden,
> Me thinkes I see a thing, arm'd with a Rake
> That seemes to strike at me.

Though Ferdinand and the Cardinal are too complex to be thought of as caricatures, they can with some justice be seen as "humorous" (see 1.1.499) in the sense that Ben Jonson uses the word. Ferdinand lives a life of physically oriented passion, whereas the Cardinal controls his physical appetites, and if he has a passion, it is a passion for the power that can be achieved by the manipulation of others through the exercise of wit.

The importance of seeing the imbalance of the brothers in terms of the excessive dominance of the body or the mind emerges when we examine the ways in which they destroy themselves in the final act of the play. Most obviously, when the power of reason (which he has rejected) leaves Ferdinand, he becomes a beast, less than human and, in Ulysses' phrase, the wolf does at last "eat up himself." The symmetry of action and consequence is illustrated further when Ferdinand denies himself the use of sight, the sense which above all feeds the soul rather than the body, and vows never to see the Duchess again (3.2.136, 141). When he breaks his vow by looking on her face after her death, it is not only his eyes which dazzle but his wits, for it is from this scene that he lapses into a deeper darkness of the mind: "I'll goe hunt the Badger, by Owle-light: / 'Tis a deed of darknesse." Ferdinand does show physical, though irrational, courage in the moment of his death, but this emphasizes the way in which his death is brought about by his unbalanced personality; he reaches for immortality, but it is an immortality of physical pleasure: "I will vault credit [a phrase explained by Lucas (in his edition) as 'overleap rational expectation'], and affect high pleasures, / Beyond death." Ferdinand never achieves self-awareness— never sees himself—and as the sight of the Duchess deprives him of his mental balance, so the meeting with Bosola, whom he has also ordered out of his sight, leads to his death.

It is the Cardinal's fondness for intrigue that brings about his downfall. Like Marlowe's Barabas and Shakespeare's Claudius before him, the Cardinal devises an ingenious plot to resolve himself of his difficulties, in this case the secrecy needed to "conuay / *Julias* body, to her owne Lodging." The action of the final scene is in some ways distinctly reminiscent of the black comedy of *The Jew of Malta,* where Barabas, after being "very busy" with a hammer, is caught literally in his own engine; the Cardinal cries for help in earnest, while his cries are the subject of jests from the onlookers above. He lacks, however, the passionate defiance of Barabas, who dies with his tongue still cursing, for he is shown to be a physical coward, howling for help, and pleading to Bosola for mercy. Unlike his brother, however, he is at least conscious of the extent of his defeat, for he asks to be "layd by, and neuer thought of," a request which may have some sense of humility, in contrast to the consistent pride and aggrandizement of his character earlier in the play. Neither brother repents; Ferdinand dies in the delusion that physical pleasure will continue after death, while the Cardinal seems to accept death as the end, with neither punishment nor reward to come. Both, in other words, reject the existence of the soul even in the moment of death.

The pattern we see in the life and death of these two characters is not far removed from melodramatic poetic justice, though it would be unfair to Webster to suggest that the play was conceived in simple black and white terms. The most effective image to describe the pattern of retribution is found in the last words of Ferdinand:

> Whether we fall by ambition, blood, or lust,
> Like Diamonds, we are cut with our owne dust.

In context the words are ambiguous, for he seems to be blaming his sister for the deaths, seeing her as part of his own dust, as in life she was part of his blood. But the image reaches beyond its context to provide an emblem for the destruction of personalities as hard, brilliant and intense as the Arragonian brothers, for it is these same qualities which are responsible for their downfall. Further, the cutting of the diamond can be seen in a contrastingly positive sense, for it is only by cutting that the diamond realizes its true brilliance and purity, and in this way the image can also be applied to the fate of the Duchess.

If we are to believe Antonio's judgement of the Duchess in his role of chorus, before he has been attracted (seduced, perhaps) into the action of the play, she is a complete woman. He singles out in turn her "discourse" or intelligence, her "sweete countenance," physical beauty, and her "noble vertue." It is not difficult to show that she combines wit and passion, though in the action which follows her virtue is by no means above reproach. She takes an obvious delight in physical pleasures. At the beginning of the play we are told that she has been indulging in "chargeable Reuels" involving masques, and she herself uses the "triumphs" and "large expence" as an excuse to call for her steward, Antonio. Her sexual warmth is shown not only in her decision to take a husband at all, but in the scenes where she woos Antonio.

> This is flesh, and blood, (Sir,)
> 'Tis not the figure cut in Allablaster
> Kneeles at my husbands tombe,

and also when they are seen in the brief domestic interlude before she is surprised by Ferdinand, where for a moment she is unknowingly flirting with her brother. Later in the confrontation between them it is her appeal that she has "youth / And a little beautie" which precipitates Ferdinand's vow never to see her more (3.2.139–40). Like Ferdinand, she possesses abundant physical courage, most notably in the same confrontation,

> 'tis welcome:
> For know whether I am doomb'd to liue, or die,
> I can doe both like a Prince,

and, of course, in the fortitude she displays in her imprisonment and torture.

Of her wit, too, there is ample evidence. She it is who plans the "politique safe conueyance for the Mid-wife," and her quick thinking "Noble Lie" gives them time and an excuse to escape to Ancona. One of the critical problems of the play is the lapse that follows where she confides in Bosola, but this, I believe, is more to be explained by a misunderstanding which is the result of a partial, but deceptive insight into Bosola's nature than by a lack of intelligence. (The reason for her disastrous error is discussed later in this essay.) The Duchess shows capacity for plotting not notably inferior to the Cardinal's and perhaps has the same tendency to overreach herself.

Whether Antonio is right in praising the Duchess's virtue is less clear. There has been a good deal of argument about the judgement a contemporary audience would have made of the Duchess's action in disobeying her brothers and marrying a man of inferior social status. It is hardly possible, in any case, that anyone in Webster's audience would have retained the attitude of rigid censoriousness we find in Webster's source:

> You see the miserable discourse of a Princesse loue, that was not very wise, and of a gentleman that had forgotten his estate, which ought to serue for a loking glasse to them which be ouer hardie in making of enterprises, and doe not measure their abilitie with the greatnesse of their attemptes.
>
> <div align="right">(William Painter, <i>The Palace of Pleasure,</i> 1567)</div>

Webster makes it clear in the intensity of the brothers' injunction to the Duchess not to remarry that they are forcing an unnatural restraint upon her, asking her to forgo the complete life that marriage offers. Ferdinand specifically asks that she repress her sensuousness: "they are most luxurious / Will wed twice"; he speaks of "those ioyes / Those lustfull pleasures" she must avoid; and he concludes his admonitions with the most startling double entendre in the play:

> FERDINAND. And woemen, like that part, which (like the Lamprey) Hath neu'r a bone in't.
> DUCHESS. Fye sir:
> FERDINAND. Nay, I meane the Tongue . . . farewell, lusty Widowe.

The Duchess's response to this is to risk her honour for the sake of marriage. She says herself that she must forsake virtue, and for the sake of her passion use stratagems and indirections:

> As a Tyrant doubles with his words,
> And fearefully equiuocates: so we
> Are forc'd to expresse our violent passions
> In ridles, and in dreames, and leaue the path
> Of simple vertue.

The effect on the Duchess of her imprisonment, torture and death is very different from the lack of dignity and lack of self-knowledge which characterize the deaths of her brothers. The tortures, added by Webster to the plot as he received it from his source, are further variations on the pattern of mental and physical imbalance, for Ferdinand is concerned to destroy the Duchess's body and mind. The Duchess's strength, which Ferdinand interprets as a "strange disdain," has the opposite effect from the obstinacy of her brothers in their deaths, for she responds to madness by a defiant sanity,

> Nothing but noyce, and folly
> Can keepe me in my right wits, whereas reason
> And silence, make me starke mad

and she responds to her physical captivity by a sharpened awareness of the sensuality she is unable to express, as Bosola tells Ferdinand:

> This restraint
> (Like English Mastiffes, that grow fierce with tying)
> Makes her too passionately apprehend
> Those pleasures she's kept from.

The grotesque torment of the artificial figures of Antonio and the children is no doubt intended by Ferdinand to bring her to despair since Antonio's death will deny her physical pleasure, and the token of the dead hand (apart from darker connotations of witchcraft) emphasizes again the sense of touch, the basest of the senses. Ferdinand judges her by his own perceptions for he assumes that her love is physical lust and her lover a lecher (see 3.2.98–100). But the love of the Duchess for Antonio and her children is not so limited, and her pain is correspondingly greater than Ferdinand could imagine. I do not see her desire to curse the stars (4.1.96) as hysteria and self-pity, for there seems to be too clearly a quality of self-irony in her awareness of the inefficacy of the curse; but I do think that her refusal to pray is a measure of the depth of her suffering and marks the moment in which she comes closest to despair, for from this point the tortures refine rather than debase her. The masque of madmen, who are all, like Ferdinand, obsessed with the bodily functions, and the last attempt by Bosola to bring her "by degrees to mortification," lead, paradoxically, to sanity and the affirmation of her living self. There is a minor, but moving symmetry in the last two encounters of Bosola and the Duchess. When the Duchess curses the stars and world to "its first chaos," Bosola mockingly reminds her of the undeniable truth that "the Starres shine still"; when Bosola denies the value and beauty of the human body, "a salvatory of green mummy . . . fantastical puff paste." and so on, the Duchess, now as unmoved as the stars she had cursed, affirms the truth of her self, both in status and in her stage presence, which must still retain a little beauty: "I am Duchesse of *Malfy* still." Tortured in mind and body, the Duchess reveals the strength and beauty of both. Further, after the despair induced in her by the sight of Antonio and the children dead, she reasserts the "continence" and virtue praised by Antonio at the beginning of the play:

> I haue so much obedience, in my blood,
> I wish it in [my brothers'] veines, to do them good.

She shows concern for her children, and is the only character in the play to die kneeling, thinking specifically of immortality. But although the Duchess has learned Christian humility and obedience, the fire of her character is in no way dimmed; one point ignored by those who emphasize the conversion of the Duchess to a state of grace in order to establish a moral core in the play is the fact that she ends her life with a fine flash of scorn for those who have so brutally tested her integrity:

> Go tell my brothers, when I am laid out,
> They then may feede in quiet.

That the Duchess is far from being merely passive in her death is illustrated by the contrast with Antonio in *The Merchant of Venice*, whose response to Shylock's "justice" is resignation:

> I do oppose
> My patience to his fury, and am arm'd
> To suffer with a quietness of spirit
> The very tyranny and rage of his.
>   (5.1.10–13)

Later he sees himself as a "tainted wether of the flock / Meetest for death" (ll. 114–15), a pessimistic image of himself which the Duchess most certainly does not share. It is interesting, incidentally, that Shylock, like Ferdinand, is "wolvish," and that Gratiano comes close to seeing metaphor as literal fact when he suggests that Shylock is a reincarnated wolf (ll. 73, 130–38).

The death of the Duchess is made the more affecting because it is far more than a simply passive, self-deprecating acceptance of tyranny, for even at the moment of death she is scornful of the evil that destroys her. The diamond shines brighter for being cut, and contrasts brilliantly with the darkness of the world around it.

Other symmetries reach out from the Arragonian triangle at the centre of the play. There is Julia, whose lust prompts her to use her wit in a dangerous and self-destructive cause; she is above all a foil to the Duchess, who could be accused of the same fault in a lesser degree, and the semi-comic scene (5.2) where she seduces Bosola is a close parallel to the romantic, half-blushful wooing of Antonio by the Duchess (compare the respective weapons, ring and pistol).

Antonio is something of a puzzle. He is described by the Duchess as "a compleat man," but he is obviously not, for he lacks both courage and wit at crucial moments in the play, and relies on Delio and the Duchess to extricate him from difficulties. The Cardinal considers him "too honest" to be a spy, he claims himself to have "long seru'd vertue, / And neu'r tane wages of her," and Bosola, at a vital moment in the plot which causes the Duchess to confide in him, describes Antonio in glowing terms, par-ticularly as "too honest." But on the other hand he becomes willingly embroiled in deceit (their escape to Ancona ironically involves his dismissal for supposed dishonesty), is thought to grow "to infinite purchase / The leaft-hand way," and above all he yields, possibly unwillingly, to a course of action which can be interpreted as excessively ambitious. Though An-tonio's ambition is stressed far more strongly by Painter, it is not neglected by Webster:

> ANTONIO. Ambition (Madam) is a great mans madnes,
> >   . . . But he's a foole
> > That (being a cold) would thrust his hands i' th' fire
> > To warme them.

And the "saucy and ambitious devil" that dances in the Duchess's ring is conjured away neither by Antonio's finger nor by what it symbolizes, witty though the suggestion is.

The key to Antonio's ineptitude is perhaps that he is both passive and naïve. He starts the play as a chorus, an onlooker, and it is something of a surprise when he steps from the audience to play a part, at the call of the Duchess. His relationship with her is at all times that of a rather bewildered follower. Particularly when they decide to part (at the Duchess's insistence) we see his passive acceptance of events. "Man (like to *Cassia*) is prou'd best, being bruiz'd.'' I suspect that the Duchess is remembering and rejecting his passivity when she responds to Bosola's remark, "The manner of your death should much afflict you," by asking, "What would it pleasure me . . . to be smothered / With Cassia?" The irony of Antonio's death is not so much that he is killed by Bosola, who was seeking to protect and vindicate him, but that he dies as the result of the one positive action he makes during the play, his attempt to confront the Cardinal unexpectedly, in an effort to duplicate the shock of Ferdinand's surprise visit to the Duchess (5.2.64–72). The extreme naïvety of this plan is underscored by Delio's sensible attempts at dissuasion, and by Antonio's almost wistful hope, "Could I take him at his prayers, / There were hope of pardon"; when the Cardinal enters at the beginning of the next scene, he is not praying, but dismissing theological speculation and conscience as "tedious." J. R. Brown suggests that Bosola's sarcastic attack on Antonio, "Euery small thing, drawes a base mind to feare," is accurate, and that Antonio has, at a deeper level, a love of fear. Certainly the Duchess says as much when she is overheard by Ferdinand; speaking, she supposes, to Antonio, she speculates on his reasons for not keeping to his own bed and puts these words in his mouth: "you'll say / Loue mixt with feare, is sweetest." If Antonio is drawn to fear earlier in the action, it is a small step to suggest that his plan to confront the Cardinal is attractive not only because it is terrifying, but because it is suicidal, and indeed when Bosola strikes him down, he sees death as a "benefit": it is appropriate that a character so negative as Antonio should seek his own death. In his dying speech Antonio, rather curiously for one who professed to serve virtue, makes no mention of the rewards of Heaven, even when he hears that the Duchess and their other children are already dead; instead he denies the value of the two pursuits in his life with which the Duchess is associated—the "Quest of Greatness" which he dismisses as equivalent to chasing bubbles, and "Pleasure of life" which is described in negative terms as a relative absence of pain, "the good houres / Of an Ague." His final injunction to his son to "flie the Courts of Princes" is profoundly negative in context, for (setting aside the possible problems of the Duchess's child by her first marriage) it is Antonio's son who gives whatever hope can be seen in the climax of the play.

Antonio's function, like Julia's, seems to be to serve as a foil to the Duchess, and to emphasize her warmth, wit, and courage by his absence of these qualities. There is a bitterly ironic symmetry in the deaths of the two: the Duchess is told in her last moments that Antonio and the eldest son are, after all, still alive, and she dies with the word "mercy" on her lips, pleading, we may suppose, for Antonio, since her own life is past help, whereas Antonio is told as he dies that the Duchess, whom he had hoped was yet alive, is murdered. Antonio dies in passive despair at the news of death, while the Duchess dies actively interceding after hearing ironically hopeful news of life.

The character who brings about the deaths of both the Duchess and Antonio, Daniel de Bosola, is of paramount importance in the play if we are in any way to see an overall pattern, for his is the major stage presence in the last act, after the death of the Duchess. The fifth act of *The Duchess of Malfi* has problems very similar to those of the fifth act of *Antony and Cleopatra,* where, after Antony's death, the play moves at a leisurely pace to a second catastrophe in the death of Cleopatra. To avoid anticlimax, the dramatic character of Cleopatra must be given weight at least equal to Antony's. His downfall is readily perceived to be tragic, the inevitable decay of a noble mind seduced by the passions of the body, but the tragedy of the seducer is a more complex affair, and it is the complexity of Cleopatra's character that sustains the final act of the play. In *The Duchess of Malfi* Bosola takes the same structural role as Cleopatra, and he also shows some of her ability to confuse and fascinate. The one common critical opinion of Bosola is that his character is ambiguous.

Since Bosola takes over the centre of the stage from the Duchess, one way of approaching his role is to see it in relation to the character he supersedes, the Duchess, whom he kills, and whose death he then paradoxically becomes concerned to revenge. If Bosola has a "humour" it is more complex than those of the Arragonian brothers, for wit and passion are both present in his character, though the role he chooses to play emphasizes his scheming since he is in effect feeding his body by the exercise of his wits—he has suffered sufficient physical privation in the galleys.

Nevertheless he shows a capacity for sensuous perception more than once in the play, particularly in his response to the moment of recovery of the Duchess:

> She's warme, she breathes:
> Vpon thy pale lips I will melt my heart
> To store them with fresh colour . . .
> . . . her Eye opes,
> And heauen in it, seemes to ope, (that late was shut)
> To take me vp to mercy.

Later, he responds to Julia's proposal with relief, amusement and interest for some time before he realizes that she can be useful to him. Bosola has a wider range of response, intellectual and emotional, than Ferdinand, the

Cardinal or Antonio, and indeed the only character who bears comparison with him in this respect is the Duchess herself.

Bosola's image of himself is that he is a realist in a world that is plagued by self-deception. The set-pieces in which he rails against "eminent" court-iers and "painting" or "scuruy face-physicke" are obvious examples in-cluded at the risk of dramatic disunity. He responds to Ferdinand's gift of gold with the accurate and sardonic assumption that his service is being bought—"whose throat must I cut?"—and his intention in accepting the role of spy is to use the brothers for his own advancement, as he says, to "hang on their eares like a horse-leech, till I were full, an[d] / Then droppe off." Bosola does not, however, avoid the shortcoming he castigates in others, for he is far less a realist than he would believe. A more accurate description of his actions would be to say that they are those of a disillu-sioned idealist, one who is never totally convinced of the supremacy of the evil he serves, and who never fully understands its workings. He has dis-covered that virtue goes unrewarded—"Miserable age, where onely the reward / Of doing well, is the doing of it"—so he assumes that evil receives fairer payment. When he decides to reveal the name of the Duchess's hus-band to her brothers he gloats, "now for this act, I am certaine to be rais'd," and after the death of the Duchess, when he perceives that Ferdinand is in danger of "falling into ingratitude," he demands "the reward due to [his] seruice." The interchange which follows dwells on justice and injustice, as Ferdinand uses the injustice of the Duchess's death as a means of refusing Bosola his pension, and Bosola, almost naïvely clinging to the concept of honour among thieves, cries, "The Office of Iustice is peruerted quite / When one Thiefe hangs another." Bosola discovers belatedly that the service of evil is no better rewarded than the service of virtue. A castigator of self-deception in others, he deceives himself when he thinks of himself as a realist; compared to Flamineo or Thersites, Bosola has an obstinate belief in justice, and, although he tries to make evil his good, he has a consistent moral sense throughout. When Antonio comments that Bosola

> rayles at those things which he wants,
> Would be as leacherous, couetous, or proud,
> Bloody, or enuious, as any man,
> If he meanes to be so:

he sees a truth he does not fully understand, for the quality Bosola is most scornful of, and perhaps equally desires, is honesty. If we see him as a corrupted idealist less corrupt than he himself believes, many of his ap-parently contradictory actions become understandable and consistent.

C. G. Thayer has shown that Bosola's ambiguities become integral to the play, rather than perplexing, if we see him in the role of a conscious actor, choosing roles as a means of reconciling his contradictory impulses. The impulse that causes him to choose a particular role is not, however, a simple desire for material gain, though the role of intelligencer is overtly chosen for this reason. Rather, Bosola's instinct seems to be to choose a role in reaction against those to whom he is speaking. To Antonio, whom he sees as simple and honest, he is cynical and sarcastic, while to Ferdinand he presents arguments of reason, moderation and compassion. His response to the Duchess is more complex, since she shares some of his obstinacy and changes her role by reacting in a similar way against the pressures placed upon her. The first major confrontation between them occurs at one of the crises of the play, when the Duchess devises a means whereby Antonio can escape but, moments later, confides fatally in Bosola. At this point Bosola considers the Duchess to be at least as corrupt as her brothers, and in the process of adding an unjust treatment of Antonio, whom he sees as a scapegoat, to the shameful lust attested by her earlier pregnancy. In Antonio's disgrace he sees the image of his own earlier unrewarded virtue, and it is not surprising that he reacts against the Duchess as he reacts against Ferdinand, with bitter scorn at those who have deserted Antonio, and an eloquent plea for the fallen man's honesty. There is a further ironical symmetry in this scene, for the Duchess has herself adopted an uncharacteristic role: as a means of escaping the tyranny of her brother, she acts the part of the tyrant towards Antonio, summarily dismissing him from her service, and it is this adopted role that Bosola is reacting against. If we are to find any plausibility in the sudden decision of the Duchess to confide in Bosola, that is if we are to see it as anything but an unexpected and uncharacteristic lapse, we must assume that Bosola's defence of Antonio is spoken with a genuine conviction, and that the Duchess responds to a truth, however temporary, rather than a falsehood. The next time they meet the roles are reversed; the Duchess defends Antonio with arguments identical to those earlier advanced by Bosola—merit and virtue are more important than pedigree—but he again reacts against such idealism by cynicism. "A barren, beggerly vertue." In a similar manner, Bosola is able to react against the obstinacy of the Duchess, when, instead of praying, she chooses to curse the stars, and yet he is able to be moved by her patience and fortitude under torture.

The combination of the example of virtue set by the Duchess in her death and the example of evil set by Ferdinand's rejection of his service has a profound effect on Bosola, though his convictions and his personality remain in essence unchanged. From this point he serves neither evil, which has betrayed him, nor virtue, which the Duchess's example shows to be admirable but passive. The main difference in Bosola from the moment of the death of the Duchess is that he changes from one who plays an essentially passive role—the tool of others, the intelligencer, the agent—to one who takes an active and decisive part in events. He still pursues his passion, justice, but, rather than waiting for justice to be meted to him as a result of his service, virtuous or evil, he takes the sword of Justice (5.2.345) into his own hands. One result is that a major theme of the fifth act of the play is the familiar moral debate between mercy and justice.

The debate is not, however, carried on between equal voices, for the one dying word of the Duchess (and her life has not obviously been connected with mercy before her death) can hardly be said to balance the entire fifth act of the play. In *The Merchant of Venice* the dramatic equality of Shylock and Portia is much closer, but even in that play the romantic optimism of the love-theme is insufficient to outweigh a sense of the inadequacy of a simple appeal to mercy in the human context, for Portia, despite her eloquence, is forced to use law to defeat law, even as the "Devil" Shylock quotes scriptures for his purpose (1.2.99), and the balance between justice and mercy in Shylock's punishment is at least open to question.

Bosola is well aware that the path he takes is not the same as the virtuous sufferance shown by the Duchess in her death, for it is just after he has spoken of what in Christian terms is the paradox of "a most just revenge" that he is reminded forcibly of her: "Still me thinkes the Dutchesse / Haunts me." Later he rewords a popular Senecan sentiment in a way that shows clearly his rejection of the Christian trust in the justice of God:

> *We value not desert, nor Christian breath,*
> *When we know blacke deedes, must be cur'de with death.*

The fallibility of the human attempt to achieve justice is shown a few lines later when he finds that the sword does not "fall right" and he kills Antonio by accident. It is perhaps only in his dying moments that Bosola realizes that the last word of the Duchess was an injunction, not a plea, though even here his mind is fixed on justice rather than mercy:

> Let worthy mindes, nere stagger in distrust
> To suffer death, or shame for what is iust.

The emphasis is upon *suffering* death and shame, in contrast to the course he took, which was actively to mete out death and shame in an ill-fated attempt to achieve justice. At the last he realizes that, compared to the

Duchess, his was "another voyage": she leads initially a life that is active and headstrong, choosing to "leaue the path / Of simple vertue," but later learns obedience and humility, enhancing rather than destroying that "integrity of life" that so distinguished her from her humorous brothers; Bosola begins passively as a tool of others—for, however much he may react against those who come in contact with him, he is as much chained to service as he was when he was in the galleys—but later tries to take a more active role in his attempt to enforce justice in his erstwhile masters. The Duchess accepts at the end of her life what Bosola rejected before the action of the play begins:

> I am acquainted with sad misery,
> As the tan'd galley-slaue, is with his Oare.

A final contrast can be seen in the effect of their deaths, for the Duchess leaves an echo in the minds of the remaining characters as well as a literal echo on stage, whereas Bosola dies in the belief that

> We are onely like dead wals, or vaulted graues
> That, 'ruin'd, yeildes no echo.

The diametrically and symmetrically opposed development of Bosola and the Duchess, two characters who are otherwise alike in their resistance to pressure and in the completeness of their response to life, is an important part of the pattern which provides overall thematic unity to the play. The other characters are those whose fragmented and incomplete view of themselves and the meaning of their lives leads them to their destruction, cut with their own dust, whether their actions are positive and active—as with Ferdinand and the Cardinal—or negative and passive, as with Antonio. These characters all pursue their lives with single-mindedness and limited self-knowledge, and the moment of their deaths defines the nature of the wasted life rather than inspiring any change of heart. Bosola and the Duchess seek to find a balance, an integration of the self, by exerting themselves against the forces that act most strongly against them; both are refined and rendered more self-aware—in the metaphor of the diamond, cut to greater brilliance—by the suffering they undergo, though Bosola's must remain a flawed brilliance, even at the end. The death of the Duchess stimulates a response most powerfully of pathos, for she alone puts her trust in Heaven, and learns to suffer rather than to resist; the tragedy of Bosola's death is stronger in a sense of terror, because he has tried to achieve justice in human terms, but fails, despite his skill and his awareness of the difficult balance he must maintain:

> I must looke to my footing;
> In such slippery yce-pauements, men had neede
> To be frost-nayld well: they may breake their neckes else.

Balance in *The Duchess of Malfi* is shown to be a condition of survival for the moral, the intellectual, and the physical self. The world in which such balance is to be sought, however, is by no means the simple, ordered world in which slippery ice-pavements occur only when a person steps outside his allotted place. Like *Troilus and Cressida, The Duchess of Malfi* has a key speech on degree—Antonio's encomium on the French court—but the wider concern of both plays is the self-destruction of disorder, the death and disease which spread through the land as a result of some "curs'd example." But as the conclusion of *Troilus and Cressida* offers small hope of the restoration of order, so the end of *The Duchess of Malfi* inspires little confidence. I cannot put much faith in the young son of the Duchess and Antonio, a character who, unlike Giovanni in *The White Devil,* speaks not a line in the play, and who was unimportant enough for Webster to leave a confusion concerning the existence of an older half-brother by the Duchess's previous marriage. If *The Duchess of Malfi* remains morally ambiguous, it is an ambiguity very similar to that which is expressed in Bosola's character, for Webster avoids a categorical didacticism by constructing a play which is the symmetrical interplay of opposites and similarities. Like Bosola, too, Webster may be reacting against idealism, for the darkness of his viewpoint could be seen as a response to the facile optimism of a play like *The Atheist's Tragedy* (*ante* 1611), in which human justice is achieved and a destructive force very like that exercised by the Arragonian brothers is defeated only by a comically improbable slip of the executioner's axe. The hard-learned and living humility of the Duchess is in marked contrast to the pious passivity of Charlemont, and the tragedy of her fate more morally acceptable than the end of *The Atheist's Tragedy*. Charlemont both has and eats the cakes of patience, "the honest man's revenge," and the material possessions scavenged by D'Amville. Webster's world is dark, for no character is able to keep his footing; but if his moral viewpoint is ambiguous, it is an ambiguity dictated by honesty. He rejects the simple answer, and builds instead a world of doubt and question, balancing one half-answer against another in a structure which is at once complex and convoluted, yet illuminated by surprising symmetries, both in the way one character is balanced against another, and in the balance which the more sympathetic characters try to maintain in themselves.

The Landscape of Imagination in *The Duchess of Malfi*

Leslie Duer

"Wish me good speed," says the Duchess of Malfi in a famous speech, "For I am going into a wilderness / Where I shall find nor path nor friendly clewe to be my guide"(1.2.323–26). The wilderness she has in mind is certainly trackless, perhaps a wasteland, but devoid neither of feature nor of life. In fact, she will eventually set out on a journey from Amalfi to Ancona, whence she will be brought back again—a journey which will be real enough, but not the journey she has in mind when she speaks to Cariola. The journey she proposes then begins with a form of marriage to Antonio, and will lead through another landscape altogether.

Of course, the most noticeable thing about realistic landscape in *The Duchess of Malfi* is that there is so little of it. *The Duchess of Malfi* is a very enclosed, very claustrophobic play. The play is set indoors or at night, and very often both indoors and at night. With one exception, the characters do not look out on anything while they are on stage. That exception is the "echo" scene, and there the view is circumscribed by a ruined wall, a "peece of cloyster" (5.3.4). There the echo may suggest, as elsewhere walls and darkness suggest, that any landscape on which one might look will be an inward one.

But while there is rarely a landscape of any sort before the eye, there is very often one before the mind's eye. To begin with, this landscape is invoked by image and metaphor and in that role is introduced by Antonio, newly returned from France. The French king, he says, considers "duely that a Princes Court / Is like a common Fountaine, whence should flow /

From *Modern Language Studies* 10, no. 1 (Winter 1979–80). © 1980 by the Northeast Modern Language Association.

Pure silver droppes in generall," (1.1.12–14). That is what the French king thinks, and it is clear that in his mind's eye Antonio sees the admirable French court in just this way. The simile is as judicious as its royal origi-nator. Cool as the "pure silvers droppes," it is part of the rhetoric of an educated gentleman for the decoration of his speech and the elucidation of his thought.

The contrast between France and Amalfi is drawn almost immediately by Bosola, speaking to Antonio of the Cardinal and the Duke. "They are like Plumtrees (that grow crooked over standing-pooles) they are rich and ore-laden with Fruite, but none but Crowes, Pyes, and Catter-pillers feed on them. Could I be one of their flattring Panders, I would hang on their ears like a horse-leech, till I were full, and then droppe off . . . What creature, ever fed worse, then hoping Tantalus?" (1.1.50–58). Bosola's language is more violent than Antonio's and his image is the more im-mediate because Bosola is in it and of it. Moreover, it is fluid and surreal: dark and crooked trees, laden with over-ripe plums and growing by a pool of stagnant water, dissolve to men and beasts, a monstrous leech hanging "on their ears" and filling itself on their blood as do the caterpillars on the pulp of the plums. Then the caterpillar/leech dissolves in turn to Bosola himself, Tantalus to the neck in corrupt water, reaching for the fruit among the magpies and the insects. Over the whole may be thought to hang the mingled odors of sweetness and corruption, the smell of death.

The image has a horrific vitality. Its impact comes not only from the force of the language in which it is put, but as well from its instability. Unlike Antonio's image, Bosola's will not stay where it belongs. Instead, invading what is established in the play as ordinary reality, it takes on for a moment a disturbing reality of its own, but does not supplant that reality with which it interferes.

This effect in *The Duchess of Malfi* has been associated persuasively with the techniques of a special form of Renaissance perspective painting, in which interleaved and distorted images yield themselves according to the position of the observer, but here our concern with this effect will be chiefly with the extraordinary result of repeated blows to the credibility of reality at its most ordinary level. Bosola's rendering of the brothers is the first of these blows, and coming as early in the play as it does, seems to suggest a general frame or context—because of the Duchess's remark and Bosola's image, I have preferred *landscape*—for the subsequent pattern of discovery in the play. Here, it seems to suggest, is Amalfi, where you think you are; but here too is the wilderness, where in fact you stand.

The notion of a known landscape is itself made metaphor in the maps by which humans seek to command the settings in which they find themselves. We want to know where we are in this most basic sense, just as we want to know where we are in more elaborated and complex senses. Because of this, the word *lost* seems still to hold resonances of terror. In art, the most profound shocks can come from the discovery that things are not what they seem. The same might be said about life, although—fortunately— life does not so often concentrate the discovery. One rather ordinary analogy for this experience might be the moment when a landscape assumed to be familiar is realized to be nothing of the sort. In *The Duchess of Malfi,* the analogue is the dawning perception of a surrealist landscape, an immanent wilderness of the spirit, which has begun to invade and displace the objective Amalfi with which the play began.

The discovery of Amalfi's wilderness comes in fragments, and is never either coherent or complete. It can be neither because it is never glimpsed wholly, and because coherence and completion would imply an order which it is not Webster's business to suggest. Bosola places at its center a stagnant source of infection, just as Antonio placed at the center of the court of France the cool, clear water of wisdom. Ferdinand supplies a further detail. His sister, as he tells her, lives "in a ranke pasture, here i' the Court" (1.1.260). "Ranke" because overgrown and disordered, it is a rank pasture too in being grossly rich to the point of surfeit, and in both odour and aspect corrupt, foul, and festering. In this Ferdinand echoes Bosola's vision of the plum trees, "ore-laden" with fruit. Here is a pastoral landscape in which even the grass is corrupt, as are the trees and the standing water which, one might fancy, lie at the center of it. What might appear at a distance as a settled landscape is upon inspection a moral wilderness; and just as in the court of France order spreads outward from a judicious king so here disorder spreads from a center which, as Bosola has pointed out, is grown corrupted.

It is an old saw that where passion is ascendant in the ruler, order is threatened. In the ruling family of Amalfi, the passions are various. That of the Cardinal is—like Vaughan's Statesman—for power, and about it he is coldly sensual. It is almost certain that Ferdinand's sanity is threatened by an inadmissible desire for his sister. And she, pursuing Antonio like a shepherdess her swain, is least of all "judicious." Commanded by her heart, she is brave and resolute. Because of this, she grasps the imagination; but that should not obscure the fact that she is commanded by will and not by wisdom as, with heroic language, she proposes to set out:

> (as men in some great battailes
> By apprehending danger have achiev'd
> Almost impossible actions: I have
>   heard Souldiers say so),
> So I, through frights and threatenings,
>   will assay
> This dangerous venture
>
>   (1.1.305–9)

What is virtue in the soldier, however, may be folly in the prince.

The "dangerous venture" begins in an exchange with Antonio marked by a doubled vision that is simultaneously routine and striking. The Duchess summons Antonio on the pretext that she is to draw a will "as 'tis princes should, in perfect memory" (1.2.347–48). Asked by her "what good deed we ought to remember first" (1.2.356), Antonio replies with a piece of slightly doubtful theology. She should "begin with that first good deed i' the world / After man's creation, the sacreament of marriage: / I'd have you first provide for a good husband: / Give him all . . . your excellent self" (1.2.360–62). Asked how princely wealth might be disposed of, Antonio contracts it all to her in a way rather like that of Donne, contracting all empires to a woman. All wealth lies in her, says Antonio, and so she should give herself; but the Duchess, caught in the image with which she began and her mind still on her brother's threats, produces an unexpected wrapping for the gift: "a winding sheet." "In a cople," replies Antonio.

Love and death are familiar companions in the hoary Elizabethan jest, of which the Duchess's remark is a variant of sorts. The sexual act culminates in a "little death," the very emblem of man's fallen condition, just as is the skull which lies beneath the fairest skin, or, in *The White Devil,* in a flower pot. All of this is conventional enough, but here Webster goes a further step. Excepting those things openly contrived by the characters themselves, images of horror never exist on the stage. They are "seen" by one character or another, and are then forgotten or dismissed as "fancy merely," or they are fragments of rhetoric, the full substance of which is not grasped by those who use them. Yet every audience is convinced that these invariably prescient phenomena are, if unseen, real—and the more vivid for being summoned only to the mind's eye. Death does not stand in the Duchess's chamber, but he is nevertheless a guest at the wedding.

The conviction of the virtual presence of an image which does not seem to belong to a world conceived realistically, is achieved by a kind of orchestration of effects. In this instance, one begins with Ferdinand's assurance that "such weddings may more properly be said to be executed than celebrated" (1.2.279); but the fuller realization of the Duchess's apposite jest comes in Ferdinand's later fury, in the course of which it is explained how indeed a "cople" of sheets might become winding sheets for those who couple in them. He would, he raves, "dip the sheets they lie in in pitch or sulphur / Wrap them in't, and light them like a match" (2.5.91–92). The shock of recognition which comes from the reappearance of the image, from an echo in the hearer's memory, lends authenticity and presence to the new image. So it gains authority not only from its intrinsic power, which is considerable, but as well because it seems confirmed by the recollection of something like it heard before. Thus having acquired, like rumor, a presence which its wholly verbal condition does not justify, it becomes part of the process by which is broken down the distinction between the insubstantial creatures of the imagination and those things which before have been accepted as objectively real.

The persecution and death of the Duchess in act 4 mark a turning point for the intrusion of image into the play's realistic or ordinary level. Insofar as the horrors to which she is subjected are seen by the audience through the eyes of the Duchess, or more exactly, through the filter of their effect upon her, they can be perceived with equal vividness as both the creations of her persecutors and as the things they represent themselves to be. The sudden literal perception by which Ferdinand's "I want his head in a business" (3.5.37) brings Antonio's severed head before the imagination gives way here to a more steadily maintained sense of simultaneous reality and illusion in the waxen images of Antonio and the children. Even if one has read the stage direction, the effect upon her lends to the effigies a momentary reality, established in retrospect by the slaughter of the children and confirmed again by the Duchess's waxen body which dazzles her brother's eyes, and which for Bosola hovers briefly between life and death.

On this occasion, the issue is complicated by the physical presence of the horrific images: waxen reproductions of corpses, a dead man's hand, all the Hallowe'en paraphernalia of deliberately created horror. Looked at coolly, these things ought to have no more power to terrify than ought the peeled grape passed around a boy scout campfire and called a dead man's eyeball. In fact, this sort of taradiddle has some effect on nearly everyone. Dead men's hands and waxen corpses bring to this moment of the play a horror and a violence which belong intrinsically to them; but in the play they take their power not only from the associations of terror intrinsic to them as symbols, but as well from the preparation which has been made for their introduction. The appearance on the stage of Antonio and the children dead is the stepping over of a shadow line which separates imagination from actuality, an actualization for which the audience has been prepared by images conjured up heretofore in language only, but by now given increasing vitality particularly in contrast to the decreased rationality of the play's assertedly realistic aspects. The subsequent discovery that the images are wax at once increases their ambiguity and challenges directly the ability of the audience to distinguish even on a physical level between reality and illusion, an ability which in the theater may always be in doubt, and which is in this case further eroded when the children die in fact, thus justifying the horror their images first evoked and turning the wax form of Antonio to an omen.

One might now look again for a moment at the matter of Antonio's (severed) head wanted by Ferdinand "in a business," not only in the context of perspective painting, but as one of a series of intrusive images, brought nearly to open statement in the play, and to some degree perceived other than consciously. Thus by the accumulation of these dimly perceived things the audience is readied to accept later moments of even greater extremity. The process described seems analogous to the phenomenon of subliminal perception, which appertains to "stimuli which cannot be distinguished or perceived under the given conditions; in particular, those which, though they cannot be consciously apprehended or named (e.g., because presented for too short a time), nevertheless give rise to either conscious or unconscious stimulus-specific effects." (*Encyclopedia of Psychology*, edited by H. J. Eysenck, W. Arnold and R. Meili). The success of the analogy depends on the agreement that the images have force in two ways: in stimulus-specific effects arising from qualities proper to themselves and independent of context (e.g., the fear, horror, or disgust evoked by the image of a severed head), and as well in a cumulative effect, which may be at first only an unease of which an audience may very well be aware, but for which it cannot absolutely account. This in turn casts further doubt on the validity or believability of what may be clearly before the eye, and attacks the ability in general (as later the protean nature of the waxen images attacks it specifically) to distinguish between the imagined and the real event within the master illusion of the play. Did the Cardinal, for example, see himself in his fishpond, or Death?

The distinction is broken down in another direction through the seeming ambiguities of the "echo" scene in act 5. Antonio and Delio stand, for the first time in the play, literally in a landscape. Here are the ruins of an abbey, "naked to the injuries / Of stormy weather" (5.3.14–15); there, across the river, stands a fragment of a cloister which, as Delio says,

> Give the best Echo that you ever heard
> So hollow and so dismall, and withall
> So plaine in the distinction of our words,
> That many have supposde it is a Spirit
> That answeres.
>
> (5.3.5–9)

But Delio does not suppose what many do. He knows that the voice which some say is a spirit, is only an echo, and he says so. An inspection of the echoed lines must confirm this, for there is not one syllable returned by the echo which has not been spoken immediately before by Antonio. There is not, in other words, the slightest reason to suppose that Antonio has had any communication from his Duchess or that when he is "presented . . . a face folded in sorrow" (5.3.57), he has experienced anything more than the vivid working of his own imagination. No more, later, is there any reason to assume that the Cardinal has done more than to place the interpretation of a guilty conscience upon the reflection of himself with a rake, glimpsed in a garden pool. Death does not threaten him from a fishpond, but from his own mind.

The reflection which the Cardinal sees, and the echo which Antonio hears, define a claustrophobic limit to the internal landscape of the play. Amalfi is walled up and once the play begins, nothing is communicated from elsewhere. There are no supernatural interventions. Amalfi (with the necessary fragments of Ancona and Rome) is wholly the creation of its immured citizens. It consists of their language endlessly magnified, distorted, turned back upon itself, and images given metaphysical reality by reflection.

The images are persuasive, even when they come at second hand, because cumulatively they have come to have as much reality as the physical world the play has seemed to assert itself to represent. Underlying that world, we have come to sense another in which all are wanderers: a wilderness which is rank, overgrown, and corrupt; populated by wolves and madmen; and having at last as much vitality as that world once thought to be rational and realistic. So Ferdinand crosses the shadow line to become his own image, a corpse-devouring wolf, and so Bosola turns palazzo to charnelhouse, as he says, "in a mist, in such a mistake as I have seen / In a play" (5.5.117–18), an identification of the play as a play which is a curiosity, seeming only to deflate the moment unless it defines within the play the instant when illusion and reality have become indistinguishable.

One emerges from such a moment in tragedy with a sense of exhaustion and relief: the worst has been very bad, but it is largely over, and the threads are to be picked up. Violence having worked itself out, new beginnings may be made, even though those experiences just undergone suggest or demand an acceptance of limitation. Shakespeare is full of this sort of thing, of course: Macduff's tough-minded optimism, hints of good government under Fortinbras, young Octavius getting the bodies underground with stately expedition so as to get back to Rome and get on with the future. In *The Duchess of Malfi,* Delio sounds a similar note.

> Let us make noble use
> Of this great ruine; and joyne all our force
> To establish this young hopefull Gentleman
> In 's mother's right.
>
> (5.5.133–36)

This seems the most recognizable of dramatic moments, although Delio speaks less in the elegiac than the heroic mode—modulating more toward the end of *Henry IV, Part 2* than toward the end of *King Lear.* Yet as much as anything in the play, Delio's words are things which are and are not. Here, the whole movement of the play comes to a moment *en tableau.* Delio and his "young hopefull Gentleman," Antonio's son, bid us look upward to a better Amalfi, erected upon the great ruin of the old. In a play in which the immanence of insubstantial things and the fluidity of apparently substantial things have urged that image and substance are indistinguishable— and equally unreliable—the very stasis of this moment seems to suggest a special reality. Instead, it is the play's ultimate illusion.

The realization of that illusion is not made by the intrusion of some new and doubtful image, supplied to unhinge a reality neither more nor less strong than the echo which attacks it. Instead, an act of memory conjures another portrait from beneath this hopeful one: Antonio's bastard, supported by Delio, brought on stage at the last to contend for an Amalfi already in the hands of the Pope, and for which there is a legitimate elder claimant. The merger of illusion and reality in the final exhaustion of *The Duchess of Malfi* requires only collapse into civil war for its completion. Delio calls his hearers to that future.

It is a crucial moment because it depends upon an independently willed and unaided act on the part of the audience, although one for which all earlier images, echoes, doubts—brought to full life by the action of memory—have prepared. In this play in which every action has not simply divorced word from thing in order to divorce appearance from substance, but has made both indistinguishably doubtful, experience mocks the hope of heroic action, although perhaps not all its dignity.

Renaissance Contexts
for *The Duchess of Malfi*

M. C. Bradbrook

> In the one predominant perturbation; in the other overruling
> wisdom; in one the body's fervour and fashion of outward for-
> titude to all height of heroic action; in the other, the mind's
> inward constant and unconquered empire, unbroken, unalter'd
> with any most insolent and tyrannous affliction.
>
> (George Chapman, letter dedicatory to his translation of
> Homer's *Odyssey*, 1614)

Chapman's comparison of the *Iliad* and the *Odyssey* would serve for Webster's two great tragedies; though each might be subtitled "A Woman at
Bay," Vittoria's "heroic action" serves her worldly ambition, whilst the
courage of the Aragonian princess gives her fortitude to endure the consequences of her bid for feminine happiness and fulfilment.

The similarities in structure (Duke and Cardinal combining in punitive
alliance) should not disguise the differences. Since they have been revived,
the superiority of *The Duchess of Malfi* has ensured half-a-dozen revivals
for every one of *The White Devil*. The play was probably acted in the winter
of 1613–14, and certainly before December 12, 1614, for on that day William
Osler (who first played Antonio) died. In Webster's own day the play was
from the first regarded as his masterpiece and seems to have enjoyed a
continuous stage success. It was one of the opening plays for the Cockpit
in Court in 1635, a command performance for royalty.

From *John Webster: Citizen and Dramatist*. © 1980 by M. C. Bradbrook and George
Weidenfeld & Nicolson Ltd., London. Columbia University Press, 1980.

The crowds who thronged to Blackfriars, where the play was put on by the King's Men, were recalled nearly twenty years later by the son of old John Heminges, leader of that group. In a macabre mock-elegy for the amputation of a duelling finger, he sets a procession of poets escorting it to the banks of the Styx:

> It had been drawn and we in state approach,
> But Webster's brother would not lend a coach,
> He swore that all were hired to convey
> The Malfi duchess sadly on her way.

Webster, if only temporarily, had transferred himself from the company of his old acting friends, to regain the kind of conditions in which he could succeed. The Blackfriars (opened only three or four years earlier) led as the first indoor theatre for an adult company—one which had held together for nearly twenty years, and which cultivated a long tradition in revenge plays. Burbage, creator of Hamlet, was in the cast. Webster made full use of the intimate setting of this hall for another family tragedy—indeed one family more significantly than before, including the Household.

Throngs of coaches crowding to Blackfriars were a common cause of complaint. Visiting dignitaries, even royalty, had been seen there. What could have brought Webster to the attention of the King's Men? Possibly the printed edition of *The White Devil,* with its generous tribute to the actors and its lament for conditions at the Red Bull. Possibly the disappearance of some of their playwrights—the retirement of Shakespeare and Beaumont.

When Webster published the tragedy, the names of all the actors (with their parts) were prefixed—the first example of such a tribute. John Lowin, as Bosola, was recognized as the leading actor; Burbage played Ferdinand, Duke of Calabria, and was later succeeded by Taylor; Henry Condell played the Cardinal of Aragon and Richard Sharpe the Duchess; Nicholas Tooley, Burbage's apprentice, doubled some minor parts.

This team included both high and low in their audiences. They were used to playing at Court, but they also kept their old theatre on Bankside, the Globe, and evidently transferred Webster's play there, although some scenes needed darkness and silence. The prison scenes do not demand a small cell, but occupy the whole stage, which implies the Blackfriars.

Webster's dedication offered this play to a grandson of Lord Hunsdon, who had been the patron of the troupe in Queen Elizabeth's time. Other playwrights gave him commendatory verses; Middleton, Rowley (leader of Prince Charles's Men and a future collaborator), together with young

John Ford, from the Middle Temple, united to affirm that the work sealed Webster's immortality, Ford comparing him with the best poets of Greece or Rome. Middleton described the audience as being overcome by pity; *pity* is indeed a key word towards the end of the play, but almost always used ironically: "Thy pity is nothing of kin to thee" (4.1.135).

The story is much simpler and bolder in relief than that of Vittoria. The historic basis was at once more distant and more tenuous; Webster took it from Painter's *Palace of Pleasure* (1567), a context that did not enforce any historic stringency. This narrative source is of minimal significance in itself. The litanies of a protracted rite of royal death are built on great public occasions and draw on many literary forms, especially the two contradictory ones of funeral elegy and wedding masque. (The latter is now extinct.)

Webster developed the inverted religious ritual of the death of Brachiano and added to it complex recall not only of many books and of other literary forms, but of events from life—such great events as the funeral of Prince Henry and the marriage rites of Princess Elizabeth and the Elector Palatine in 1613, such local events as overseeing Robert Dove's charity for the condemned at Newgate. To this he joined an attention to his individual actors, and to the effects which could be achieved in his theatre, which is closer than any other dramatist, except Shakespeare, was prepared to go. He knew what could be asked of a boy who had played Hermione or Queen Katherine. Webster made his theatre into an instrument to play on, but he too had vibrated to performance before fashioning it. His use of plays that were still unpublished *(Macbeth, Othello* or *Antony and Cleopatra)* proves his attentiveness. Consequently, he shares with Shakespeare an openness to reinterpretation. This paradoxical result, rising from richness and complexity, allows a great variety of valid interpretation and emphasis. It is the reward of a performer's art. With Shakespeare, Webster attracts new relevances from the experience and cultural concern of modern audiences. For example, the modern view that the Duke of Calabria was incestuously fixated upon his twin sister can satisfactorily compensate for inaccessible Jacobean theological or social moods, just as, in a living organism, one part may take over the function of another. This adjustment is the mark of classic work, always renewable by transformation. Today, unless they have personally faced some extremity of horror and collective wickedness, very few believe in supernatural evil, or personal devils.

In this chapter therefore, first the social, then the psychological, and lastly the contemporary theatrical background are explored to reestablish the missing context—this, not to replace modern reading, but to enrich it.

The Duchess of Malfi is distinguished from *The White Devil,* which was firmly grounded in recent history, and the distinction produces a different conception of the play—one which was also influenced by the very different playing conditions at Blackfriars.

The story had survived only because it had been recounted by a contemporary, Matheo Bandello, who told it as Antonio's tragedy; this Italian bishop may have been the Delio of the play, as he seems to have known Antonio personally. Tragic "shaping," carried through the French to Painter, had made it legendary in the course of one hundred years, the interval between the murder of Antonio Bologna at Milan in October 1513 and Webster's play. The secret marriage between the young widowed Duchess and the steward of her household, their five years' happiness, their flight, and the vengeance of her brothers were told through long speeches, laments and songs from the two lovers. Painter displayed what historical records fail to supply: the Duchess's imprisonment and death by strangling, together with her faithful maid and two children; he briefly ended with the record of Antonio's assassination later on the orders of the Cardinal.

Into such a legend Webster was free to insert contemporary colour. The Spanish rulers of the Kingdom of Naples could be interpreted in the light of contemporary Spanish honour and Spanish pride. (Indeed, a few years later Lope de Vega was himself to write a play on the story of the Duchess.) There was freedom also to shape it in terms of the noblest theatrical form, the masque, though in an unusual and paradoxical way, turning the form and the occasion upside down. The old tale and the modern instance, eternity and time, were combined in Webster, and still without any dogmatic fixations. His negative capability, or "power of being in doubts, mysteries, fears without any irritable reaching after fact and reason," was strengthened by contrasts of darkness and light, diamond and mist, so that his perspectives in this piece are larger, and yet his style is softened. The sharp contrasts of the central scene in *The White Devil* have become the nightmares of the Duchess's prison in act 4. The total effect is still paradoxical—the epigrams of Bosola and the Duchess giving rise to numinous shudders, the abrupt breaks in speech to the stealthy encroachment of menacing forces, stage figures to the implications they carry. In place of the Ambassadors who represent the political aspect of Vittoria's challenge, perspectives of hell open in the Duchess's prison; since the time of Charles Lamb these scenes have been recognized as being "not of this world." Madness was itself thought of as diabolic possession, and the "comic" masque of madmen prefigures the later madness of Ferdinand.

There is no single "source." Bandello's narrative records his extreme shock, which he dealt with by blaming everybody—Antonio for his presumption, the Duchess for her lust, the brothers for their cruelty; his position is self-contradictory. For Webster's generation, the end of Penelope Rich and Charles Blount's love affair, or the story of Antonio Pérez and the Princess of Eboli, offered possible endorsement. The modern reader is at least better equipped by this analogue from Webster's day, to gain insight into the price for private security amid court splendour, and also into the psychology of the spy. For Webster's chief method of shaping the story was to create the single character of Bosola out of the Duchess's household servants, her prison tormentors, and the named assassin of Antonio in Milan, a Lombard captain. Bosola's insecurity, his bitter jesting and self-mockery, his constant, unremitting demands for "reward," which is always denied him, and finally his love of disguises as a mode of psychological relief can all be found in Pérez. Better than any other writer of his time, Webster has realized the dark side of political power, the cruel grip of intelligence networks, the shocks of betrayal. In production, Bosola often dominates the play, so that the lives of the Aragonian princelings serve but as background to his self-destruction. This spy, who repents and institutes a counter-vengeance for the murder which he himself had executed on command, reaffirms the tragic fate of the servant. The great lady who ends her days in darkness, close prisoner in her own palace, shares the pride of Penelope Rich and Ana de Mendoza, Princess of Eboli.

Every Jacobean would know that madness was hereditary in the royal blood, which it was the Duchess's crime to have contaminated by a base marriage; they would also know the story of Philip II's heir, Don Carlos, strangled in prison.

The last element of public feeling which Webster incorporated into his play may not have been recognized by his contemporaries. His own mourning for England's heir, Henry, Prince of Wales, who had died in November 1612, had been set down within a few weeks in *A Monumental Column,* his elegy. Here many of the images, later closely united in *The Duchess of Malfi,* lie about as *disjecta membra.* It is not in itself a memorable achievement, but points to one of the sources of the tragedy; this widespread national grief provided some powerful emotional drives which went into the tragedy and were transformed.

It is possible to sustain a reading of the play in terms of contemporary views of social duty or social structure; it is also perfectly possible to read it as a character study of the four leading figures, with religious overtones, or as a subtle variation upon the perspectives of the masque. The story is "open" not so much to the moral alternatives which are powerful in *The White Devil* as to differences of genre, of interpretative approach, or of emphasis, of light and shade. It has proved attractive in this way to modern poets, who have adapted it in a thoroughly Websterian fashion.

In accordance with the practice of the private theatre, Webster divides the play into five acts, centring on the Court, the bedchamber, the world, the prison and the grave. But these locations are not closely defined. In the prison scene, the waxwork show of mortification, the masque of madmen and the ritual of execution are in themselves theatrical; they belong with the hell-castle of *Macbeth,* with its porter and its alarm bell, with the shows in the witches' cave. These in turn reflect the "great doom's image" of medieval drama—Heaven and Hell. The King's Men at this time were increasing this element in their productions—with new effects in *Macbeth,* and with Shakespeare's final plays. Their own experience of the Court masque (where they had enacted the witches for the antimasque of *The Masque of Queens*) must have affected their general style. It was a secular ritual, using religious terms, but without ever introducing religious material.

The legendary, the contemporary, the dramatically ritualistic are laminated, and this inlay increases the dramatic life of the work. What now has to be substituted for Webster's contemporary lamination is something of our own day: both T. S. Eliot and Allen Tate, in their lyrics, added this perspective to the original poetry. Eliot chooses the bedchamber scene, where the Duchess is surprised, partly through Antonio's jest of leaving her, and sees in her mirror not the face of her husband but that of her brother, holding out a poniard. This is adapted so that the two figures become two aspects of one man, who both loves and hates at once. The effect is not pity but terror:

> "You have cause to love me, I did enter you in my heart
> Before ever you vouchsafed to call for the keys"
> With her back turned, her arms were bare,
> Fixed for a question, her hands behind her hair
> And the firelight shining where the muscle drew. . . .
> There I suppose they found her
> As she turned
> To interrogate the silence fixed behind her.
>
> (*The Waste Land*)

Allen Tate contrasts the tale of the Duchess with the sterility of a modern reading:

> The stage is about to be swept bare of corpses.
> You have no more chance than an infusorian
> Lodged in a hollow molar of an eohippus.

Now consideration of the void coming after,
Not changed by the "strict gesture" of your death,
Splits the straight line of pessimism
Into two infinities.

And the katharsis fades in the warm water of a yawn.
(*Horatian Epode to* The Duchess of Malfi)

If the cynicism of Bosola and Flamineo is to jest about moral values they cannot afford, Tate's persona in this poem fits into the play well enough. Its own comedy starts in the opening scene at Court; then, in act 2, Bosola uses the tone of the Malcontent in his mockery of women's painting; Ferdinand's actions begin with the manic grandeur of forbidding his courtiers to laugh except when he laughs. Later, as he silently confers with his brother, and someone comments, "The Lord Ferdinand laughs," it seems

like a deadly cannon
That lightens ere it smokes.
(3.3.54–55)

The Duchess's mirth consists of simple, rather childish bawdy jokes with her maid and her husband, but Ferdinand's entry transfers it into the bitter wit with which she enacts her play of banishing Antonio. She neither employs nor suspects any espionage; her wit serves chiefly to control her own pain and resentment and acts upon herself (as Bosola's also acts upon himself.)

Historically, the removal of Antonio Bologna and his Duchess from this world was neatly and expertly carried out; there was no scandal and little comment. It was a family affair; the Duchess simply vanished and was never seen again, her secret marriage matched by her secret death. In this play, uniquely among Webster's works, there is no trial; tyranny is condemned by Ferdinand's self-accusation:

By what authority didst thou execute
This bloody sentence?
BOSOLA. By yours—
FERDINAND. Mine? Was I her judge?
Did any ceremonial form of law
Doom her to not being? did a complete jury
Deliver her conviction up i' th' court?
Where shalt thou find this judgment registered
Unless in hell . . .?
(4.2.298–304)

The only form of sentence we have witnessed was that of her banishment from Ancona, carried out in dumb show, at the shrine of Our Lady of Loretto. This was evidently staged in great splendour, for an Italian visitor to London commented upon it in 1618. During the ceremony the Cardinal violently took her wedding-ring from the Duchess's finger, which constituted an ecclesiastical act of nullity of the contract; punishment by the secular arm (banishment) followed this ecclesiastical judgment. From the comments of the two onlookers one learns also that the Pope has seized the duchy ("But by what justice?" "Sure, I think by none / Only her brother's instigation").

In the case of Antonio Pérez and the Princess of Eboli the arbitrary nature of Spanish judicial procedure, with the unscrupulous use of ecclesiastical charges in default of secular evidence, was the whole point of the *Relaciones* being published in England. It showed to the English (including the English Catholics) the superiority of English justice. There is no form of justice in the family acts of vengeance against the Duchess, who repeatedly calls it tyranny.

If the drama were viewed simply as a family history, as it might have been by one of Webster's young friends from the Inns of Court, it would have been considered that the Aragonian brethren were lacking in a proper sense of duty in counselling the young Duchess to live unmarried, and then going off and leaving her. It was their duty to look round the world at large, find a suitable husband and present him to her. The absolute authority of the head of the family over all members was not disputed, and the natural subjection of sister to brother appears in a number of English plays. But imposing on the Duchess the heroic role of Virtuous Widow—a role which the individual could certainly choose, which was seemly for older women, which could confer extraordinary power on a Catherine de Medici—was tyrannical. Later, indeed, Ferdinand pretends he is planning a marriage with Malateste, and the Cardinal also claims to have a plan for her remarriage. Antonio, as her faithful servant, counsels marriage to her before she makes her declaration of love to him. (In all stage comedy, the remarriage of widows is a central assumption.)

Yet, whatever the value of "a contract in a chamber," the Duchess, by failing to publish her marriage, destroys her own good fame. Antonio is aware that "the common rabble do directly say she is a strumpet." To her brother she claims that "my reputation is safe," but he declares that once it is lost it is irrecoverable (3.2.116–35). He explains, as if to a child, that love is found only among shepherds or dowerless orphans. Marriage as a social contract, an affair of the larger family, means that if Antonio was her husband he was not her "lord and husband"; he jests at himself as a lord of Misrule, reigning only at night. He simply does not belong with the great ones; his role in the marriage is passive, indeed feminine; the Duchess, acting as the masculine half in the partnership, proposes the contract, directs their action, plans their flight, faces her brothers. At the end, Antonio hopes only to ask pardon of his new kinsmen. As a member of the Household, he should have respected its degrees; since he is an upper servant, his life is held as cheap as Bosola's by the brothers.

Imprisonment was the usual penalty for clandestine marriages between a great lady and a servant. The most eminent example is John Donne, secretary to the Lord Keeper, who, after he had married the Keeper's niece, Anne More, in December 1601, was two months later committed to the Fleet Prison for conspiracy to violate the civil and common law. The cleric who performed the ceremony was also jailed, as was even the man who had "given" the bride—a gift he was certainly in no position to bestow. Years of poverty followed. The case of Lady Arabella Stuart is more frequently mentioned in the context of this play; in that instance it was her nearness to the throne which caused her imprisonment.

One of the works that Webster was certainly reading at this time, for there are many "bondings" in this play, was Montaigne's essay "Upon Some Verses of Virgil" (bk. 3, chap. 5), which treats of love and marriage. Montaigne assumes, without requiring any examination, the double standard by which men would face almost any crime in their family rather than the infidelity of their wives. The particular passion of the Italians, love ("Luxury is like a wild beast, first made fierce with tying and then let loose"), is stronger in women than in men. Marriage is another thing: "Wedlock hath for his share honour, justice, profit and constancy; a plain but more general delight, Love melts in only pleasure; and truly it hath it more ticklish; more lively, more quaint and more sharp . . . a pleasure inflamed by difficulty; there must be a kind of tingling, stinging and smarting. *It is no longer love, be it once without arrows and without fire.*" Webster laminates Montaigne's cool and occasionally alarming survey of the relation between the sexes with the glowing ardour of Sidney's *Arcadia*: the perfection of its two heroines in prison, their sufferings for love. In Sidney he found the device of the wax figures used as torture for his Duchess. Florio's translation of Montaigne had been dedicated to, among others, Penelope Rich; the collision between Sidney's burnished examples of Virtue and the sardonic enigmas of Montaigne must have been strengthened by bitter contrasts in the life of a woman who linked these two works.

Penelope's last battle was for the right to call herself Countess of

Devonshire; the Duchess of Malfi is never given a personal name. She is always addressed by her title. Her private person is suppressed in her public role; we never meet Giovanna d'Aragona. Yet it is the struggle between these two elements which her maid laments in the concluding words of act 1:

> Whether the spirit of greatness or of woman
> Reign most in her, I know not, but it shows
> A fearful madness; I owe her much of pity.
> (1.1.504–6)

Webster was later to use another antithesis, in comparing "The Character of a Virtuous Widow"—who never remarried—with "An Ordinary Widow," who remarried again and again: noble and comic, sacred and risible. In this play however he showed the one character in two different roles, overt and covert. Her public role as Duchess gives her no power within the family; she makes her domestic choice with a sense that she is acting like soldiers who

> in some great battles
> By apprehending danger have achieved
> Almost impossible actions.
> (1.1.344–46)

And to Antonio she suggests that "love mixed with fear is sweetest" (3.2.66).

The Duchess of Malfi's life was cleft in two by her secret marriage; her integrity was restored ultimately by the price she was prepared to pay for it. She changes and grows, as few other characters do; and ultimately the language she uses is that of religious experience—there is nothing doctrinal about it. For she is denied the consolation of the Church (which Spaniards were always most punctilious in allowing to the victim); she has to improvise her own ceremonies. The Cardinal and Ferdinand use the ceremonies of Church and State to release their own perversions.

Tragic awakening begins for the Duchess with a pathetic variation on her brother's warning that happiness dwells only with unambitious shepherds or dowerless orphans:

> The birds that live i' the' field
> On the wild benefit of nature, live
> Happier than we; for they may choose their mates
> And carol their sweet pleasures to the spring.
> (3.5.18–21)

This is pastoral happiness that Webster drew elsewhere in his "Character of a fair and happy Milkmaid."

At parting with Antonio, she hopes that they will not part thus "i' th' Eternal Church" and sees the heavy hand of Heaven in her affliction:

> I have seen my little boy oft scourge his top
> And compared myself to 't; nought made me e'er
> Go right but Heaven's scourge-stick.
>
> (3.5.81–83)

This is not a sustained attitude, for human pride and even religious cursing at other points contradict it. Her "diamond" quality combats with her fragility: she is no stoic; conflicting passions succeed her initial stunned, somnambulistic calm.

The Hell, or Purgatory, which the Duchess undergoes in prison is defined by its remoteness or detachment. Her first words after Antonio has left her are "My laurel is all withered" (3.5.93). The laurel which protected the Roman Emperors from thunder was also their emblem of good fame. In being removed to her own palace, she enters a realm darker and grander to which she provides her own choric comment:

> I have heard
> That Charon's boat serves to convey all o'er
> The dismal lake but brings none back again.
>
> (3.5.107–9)

These Roman comments transcend her own role; they give a godlike view.

The silence of the prison scenes is preceded by Bosola's account of her own deep and silent grief. The scene may well be her own bedchamber, where she jested with Antonio, the arms of the Duchy of Malfi still blazoned on the tester. The "shows" of Antonio and the children, following the "love token" of the dead man's hand, bring her to feel that living itself is hell. She invites the ritual punishment for an ill-matched marriage:

> If they would bind me to that lifeless trunk
> And let me freeze to death.
>
> (4.1.68–69)

A deep sense of unreality has come upon her; a world "not just confused but unfathomable" is created by superimposing two images in a new "art"; the magic ring and the dead man's hand are "witchcraft"; the "show" is the preparatory stage of her tomb-making. Bosola tries to convert this to penance, rites for the dying. The madmen with their mocking jests (as if from some great court antimasque), "Woe to the caroche that brought home my wife from the masque at three o'clock in the morning; it had a large feather bed in it" (4.2.104–6), go on to babble of the Last Judgment. Their comments on sex and violence serve both as prelude to the "masque" of the Duchess's execution and also as a foretaste of the supernatural evil to be let loose at the end, when Ferdinand thinks he is transformed to a wolf and when, in storm, "the Devil rocks his own child." For a tempest marks the final holocaust.

With the inverted three actions of a true masque—the entry of the executioners, their invitation to the Duchess to join them, and their presentation of the gifts that bring "Last benefit, last sorrow"—the Duchess finds that the coffin has indeed replaced the nuptial bed; she has "welcomed" ruin before, but her new perception goes deeper:

> I perceive death, now I am well awake,
> Best gift is, they can give or I can take.
> (4.2.224–25)

Bosola has stripped her title; if she declared, "I am Duchess of Malfi still"— perhaps glancing at the scutcheon above her bed, or pointing to it—the audience might remember that the arms of those condemned to die are taken down. When this happened to Mary, Queen of Scots, she replaced her royal arms by a crucifix. Bosola's last disguise also brings him out of history into Webster's world, the parish charity for the poor prisoners of Newgate:

> I am the common bellman
> That usually is sent to condemned persons
> The night before they suffer.
> (4.2.173–74)

The ritual has brought her too out of the dream country of the Revels; it is as Giovanna Bologna that she gives instructions for the care of her children and sends a last message to her brothers—"Go, tell my brothers, when I am laid out, / They then may feed in quiet" (4.2.236–37)—as she kneels to "enter heaven." There is almost a suggestion of cannibalism latent in the image, which catches up an earlier one. When the gruesome comedy of the waiting-maid's death is ended, Bosola sees where he is—"a perspective that shows us hell"—and he names the deed as "murder."

"I am Duchess of Malfi still" had asserted the "Mind's empire" against Ferdinand's "tyrannous affliction"; Bosola replies, "That makes thy sleep so broken." Had she said, "I am Giovanna Bologna still," she would have more truthfully disclosed the way in which her marriage had severed her public role from her private person. She had "awakened" Antonio with the words "[I] only do appear to you a young widow / That claims you for her husband" (1.1.456–57) and "put off all vain ceremony"—though later she had improvised one.

For those who would see the Duchess as love's martyr, the moment of her death is crucial. Critical judgment has placed her at every point on the scale that separates Fair Rosamond or Jane Shore from the Virgin Martyr (a play on St Dorothea had just been acted at the Red Bull). The Duchess's death converts Bosola, the expected miracle. The sight of her face also "awakens" Ferdinand to what he has done: "Cover her face; mine eyes dazzle; she died young" (4.2.264). In the darkness of the prison this suggests a halo of glory; sex, violence and religion are fused in nine short words.

Antonio's first portrait of her to his friend had enskied and sainted her; yet when she finally appears to him "a face folded in sorrow" in the grave-yard, she seems only a mournful, hovering ghost, still the wife of Antonio, still earthbound.

Giovanna Bologna is buried obscurely in the ruins of an ancient mon-astery; it is as "my wife" that Antonio recognizes the voice of the Echo. The scene is highly ritualized (perhaps, as in the echo scenes in Monteverdi, Echo was sung), but this truly obscure being has been heard once before—crying out in the pains of childbirth. The unknown self within the Duchess should perhaps be heard as another voice, lacking security, a voice as home-less as the birds that once she envied for their freedom. This voice offers no comfort. He will "never see her more."

Theological security, "which some call the suburbs of hell," had be-trayed the Duchess. It is "mortal's chiefest enemy." The conviction that the future is assured, springing from the self, its good deeds or its good intentions, is the vice of the Pharisee, but also rises from that combination of Pride with Generosity that defeats Prudence. Security means an unex-amined assumption of safety, privilege and stability; it makes denial or responsibility easy, being basically both self-centred and inattentive.

Antonio knows that faithful counsellors should warn the Prince of "what he ought to foresee" (1.1.22), but when the Duchess gives him her wedding-ring, "to help your eyesight," he sees "a saucy and ambitious devil dancing within the circle," which the Duchess removes by putting the ring on his finger. She senses his "trembling." They embrace. Her words are stately or fantastic, but her blushes grow deeper, she asks him to lead her to the bride-bed. For a foil to the Duchess, Webster invented Julia, the Cardinal's mistress, who takes a man if she feels the impulse. In a parody of the Duchess's wooing she seizes Bosola by entering with a pair of pistols and asking him what love potion he has put in her drink. Her end is another macabre jest; the Cardinal poisons her by giving her his Bible to kiss.

Had the Duchess been wanton, she would have tried her arts upon her jailers; and, indeed, the nature of Bosola's devotion is very like love when, after he thinks she is killed, he finds her still living:

> She's warm, she breathes.
> Upon thy pale lips I will melt my heart
> To store them with fresh colour.
>   (4.2.341–43)

Antonio and Bosola stand almost at the same distance from Aragonian royalty; Ferdinand had thought of using Antonio as his spy, and to him there could not be very much to distinguish between the head of the house-hold servants and "some strong-thighed barge-man" or one of the porters who carried coals up to the Duchess's lodging. From his ducal height, he twice snubs Bosola for attempting to find any explanation of the spying he is set to do, offers his sister his hand to kiss, and even, in madness, deals ruthlessly with the familiarity of the doctor. The Cardinal, whom Antonio at the opening painted as a religious hypocrite, prepares to eliminate Bosola because he will not risk blackmail from one who knows him as a "fellow murderer." The hollowness of the Cardinal's priestly role is the latest rev-elation of the play. In the last scene the Cardinal and the Duke are both in prison; the Cardinal has made his own prison for himself, by locking the doors and ordering his Court not to pay any attention to cries for help. The "accidental judgments, casual slaughters" that finally leave the stage corpse-strewn are in violent contrast to the ritual of the Duchess's "last presence chamber," but they are taking place in a prison, and perhaps some lighting or "blocking," or the Cardinal's scutcheon, might relate the two scenes.

The Cardinal knows already that he is in Hell; looking in his fish-ponds for his own image, he has seen "a thing arm'd with a rake" that seems to strike at him. (It is an echo of the scene where the Duchess sees the face of Ferdinand instead of Antonio's.) The garment of those con-demned by the Inquisition was painted all over with devils, to show their state within; so the devil that threatens, as it seems from outside, is really already in possession, and pulling him down. This devil takes away the Cardinal's power to pray; he is in a theological state of despair.

The Cardinal "ends in a little point, a kind of nothing." Bosola sees his killing as an act of justice, and, in his last words, the Cardinal echoes his sister in appealing to her executioner (now his) for "Mercy." Yet he acknowledges the sentence:

> O Justice!
> I suffer now for what hath former bin—
> Sorrow is held the eldest child of sin.
>
> (5.5.53–55)

In a mockery of *L'uomo universale*, the Renaissance man, he has played many roles—shed his Cardinal's robes for the sword and armour of the soldier; endured with some boredom the attentions of a mistress for fashion's sake. His cool manipulation of finance—it is the Pope who gets the dukedom of Malfi, not Ferdinand—ruins the Duchess and the experienced Antonio.

Ferdinand has but one overt role—the secular head of the family, the soldier—and he plays it with gusto, ostentatiously. His moments of silence, of playing "the politic dormouse," and his outbursts of manic rage, build up to the madness that is demonic and fatal. Burbage, who had created the roles of Hamlet and Lear, was playing this part.

For a Jacobean, the madness of the Spanish royal house and the Spanish code of honour would have sufficed to explain all this; to a modern audience, the idea that Ferdinand's driving impulse is an incestuous fixation on his twin sister opens up a meaning more readily available today. It explains the ceremonial forms his persecution takes; ritual is an effective way of disguising and controlling repressed desires. He sees himself as a physician administering purges, even whilst he also sees the Duchess's behavior as Heaven's punishment for some sin in himself or his brother—a punishment through their common flesh:

> I could kill her now
> In you or in myself, for I do think
> It is some sin in us, heaven doth revenge
> By her.
>
> (2.5.63–66)

(The pious Marcello had the same idea.) The Cardinal replies, "Are you stark mad?" His attempts at control in the scene where he meets her, coupled with his utter refusal to listen to what she has to say, or to see Antonio, are part of the protective design by which Ferdinand seals off the interior chaos that eventually engulfs him. The ritual execution of the Duchess restores him to a sense of what he has done to "my dearest friend"—before this last insight finally destroys his mental balance. Such an explanation of

Ferdinand has been found so serviceable on the modern stage as now to be almost orthodox.

Incest was not a subject about which Jacobean dramatists felt any squeamishness. Tourneur brings it, as a threat, into *The Atheist's Tragedy*, and Webster allows the noble lover to subscribe to it in *The Devil's Law-Case*. Acting as bawd to one's own kin might be considered "a kind of incest," and, in basing a tragedy upon fraternal incest, Webster's young friend John Ford some dozen years later was to copy themes from this very play. The hero and heroine in *'Tis Pity She's a Whore* join themselves together in a private ceremony which invokes the very tie that should prevent it:

> Sister }   On my knees
> Brother }   even by our mother's dust, I charge you
> Do not betray me to your mirth or hate;
> Love me, or kill me { sister.
>   { brother.
>
> (1.2.249–55)

They are two innocents in a wicked world, and their union has the isolating effect of an addiction, like the homosexuality of Edward II in Marlowe's play. Society is uniformly disgusting, and these people have isolated themselves from it, each with one who appears the mirror of his or her self. The fraternal relation serves Ford, as it served Webster, in more than one play; its stable, immutable quality (which made one French heroine prefer her brother to her husband on the grounds that the second could be replaced, but not the first) is reflected even in the final scene, for, after entering with Annabella's heart upon his dagger, in a parody of the devotional worship of the Sacred Heart, Giovanni dies with a prayer that restores a chaste remoteness, as if he were looking into a mirror:

> Where 'er I go, let me enjoy this grace,
> Freely to view my Annabella's face.
>
> (scene 6, ll. 107–8)

"Viewing" undoes Ferdinand.

There is much in the strangling of the Duchess to recall the strangling of Desdemona, not least her momentary revival after she is supposed dead. But the remorse of Ferdinand is shared by Bosola; it is he who sees the great gulf between the "sacred innocence that sweetly sleeps on turtle's feathers" and his inner hell. Ferdinand feels his life bound up with hers; they were twins. Those who are interested to work out such matters for performance might imagine that the twins were united in enmity against their elder brother, the Cardinal; that the hidden animosity between the two men is shewn by the Cardinal's effortless use of Ferdinand as his pawn. He even usurps Ferdinand's part as a soldier, for there is nothing priestly about him except his vestments—themselves of course a sign of diabolic intrusion to the more Puritanically minded members of the English Church.

Ferdinand shares with Bosola, his spy, a capacity for pain; the pain hidden behind an outward façade is the thread of life that runs through scenes of external violence. Pain so great that it "makes us no pain to feel" became in Ford "the silent griefs that cut the heart strings"; in Ferdinand it emerges in images—sometimes poignant, sometimes bizarre:

> Thou are undone:
> And thou hast ta'en that massy sheet of lead
> That hid thy husband's bones and folded it
> About my heart.
>
> (3.2.111–14)

Or "The pain's nothing; pain many times is taken away with apprehension of greater, as the toothache with the sight of the barber that comes to pull it out" (5.5.59–61). His last words imply that he is one flesh with Giovanna—and one dust:

> My sister O my sister! there's the cause on 't.
> Whether we fall by ambition, blood or lust,
> Like diamonds, we are cut with our own dust.
>
> (5.5.71–73)

Sensitive apprehension of pain lies behind his brutality, and sharpens it, but whilst the modern reading of his impulses as incestuous allows a valid presentation, it seems probable that in Webster's day the same effect upon the audience would have been reached by different means.

Bosola, created by fusing three historic figures in a single tragic role, is sometimes felt to be unconvincing, but on stage the part becomes capable of dominating the play. Bosola is a professional murderer, prepared to kill a servant to prevent him unbarring a door; he has served as a galley-slave for murders committed at the Cardinal's instigation. Yet he is also a "fantastical scholar," slow in working, much concerned with curious learning. When he defends Antonio, as a faithful servant missing reward, and the Duchess unwarily discloses her marriage, he offers her the powerful tribute of the unbeneficed scholar's prayers. Her choice of virtue above greatness will bring her good fame from "neglected" poets, who will presumably win their own immortality from her story.

Antonio, "this trophy of a man / Raised by that curious engine, your white hand," will also be praised by poets when heralds have exhausted their easily bestowed nobility. Tributes to the Duchess from needy poets in England had in fact been provided by Robert Greene and George Whetstone (see Boklund).

But Bosola also counsels their flight should be disguised as a religious pilgrimage to Loreto (transport is his job). This proves the Duchess's undoing, for it is Papal territory. His praise is immediately followed by the sickening drop to his role as spy:

> What rests but I reveal
> All to my lord? O this base quality
> Of intelligencer!
>
> (3.2.326–28)

Bosola, the chief instrument in the Duchess's betrayal and subjection, also bears the strongest witness to her virtues. In prison he may hope, in some confused way, to save her soul if not her body from Ferdinand's damnable plan to "bring her to despair"; but there is a collusive relation between the two men that makes the servant in some way an emanation of his lord.

Ferdinand, in such utterance—or, again, when Bosola urges the need for her penance—"Damn her! that body of hers / While that my blood ran pure in 't was more worth / Than that which thou wouldst comfort, call'd a soul" (4.1.121–23)—and in the constant imagery of fire, blood and tempest that surrounds him, may be considered as diabolically possessed even before his madness takes over. This leaves Bosola also the prisoner of dark powers, tempted by devils in human form (as a "scholar," he might have been once in holy orders).

Ferdinand has sworn in the bedchamber scene that he will never see the Duchess more. When Bosola meets her it is always in some form of disguise: "vizarded" at her capture, dressed as an old man (the stage emblem for mortality), then a "tomb maker," then playing "the common bellman." Whether for their effect upon her, or for relief to himself, these disguises enable Bosola to act as a kind of priest, even whilst he conducts the execution. Yet at the end he is still asking for reward from Ferdinand; he expects to be paid the rate for the job—a pension. He is cheated by the two devils who have brought him so low.

Bosola is not the same kind of Protean shape-changer as Flamineo; his melancholy is not assumed, and his "antic dispositions" have more than a touch of Hamlet about them; but he is a Hamlet who cannot unpack his heart with words. However, his death speech is firmly orchestrated ("One can almost see the conductor's raised baton," ejaculates one critic). He begins on a low note, with the unwilling murder of "his other self," his fellow-servant and the lover of the Duchess, Antonio:

> Such a mistake as I have often seen
> In a play.
>
> (5.5.95–96)

He recollects "the dead walls or vaulted graves" where the Duchess's voice had echoed, but he hears none:

> O this gloomy world!
> In what a shadow or deep pit of darkness
> Doth (womanish and fearful) mankind live.
>
> (5.5.100–102)

He rises to a brave sentiment, but falls away as he too feels "Charon's boat" approach:

> Let worthy minds ne'er stagger in distrust
> To suffer death or shame for what is just—
> Mine is another voyage.
>
> (5.5.103–5)

Then, "staggering in distrust," he ends on this faint litotes.

He can mock his own degradation wittily—"I think I shall shortly grow the common bier for churchyards" (5.2.311–12)—yet, with all his many roles, Bosola is never permitted the luxury of being a self. He is the masquer, in both senses: he comes with ceremony to his captive Duchess; he leads those scenes that have been generally understood as parody or inversion of a Court masque. Additionally, the play, from beginning to end, depends upon varying or enlarging, contracting or inverting the forms of a masque.

The year 1613 had seen a great number of masques, in particular the three given for the marriage of the Princess Elizabeth to the Elector Palatine on St Valentine's Day 1613. Two of these masques contained antimasques of madmen. The Court masque, as developed by Ben Jonson and Inigo Jones, celebrated the splendours of the royal house by the epiphany or revelation of some great personage (usually the Queen), who carried the image of a divine or heroic being, supposed to be drawn down to inhabit a mortal frame. It was a rite of cosmic harmony, linking the government of the realm with the government of the spheres, or the marriage of some great persons with the unity of the cosmos. It was a secular sacrament. It was magic. The masquers ultimately came down from their stage to join the audience; the "revels," or dances, which ensued, preceded sometimes by the offering of gifts, were the main function of the rites.

It had long ago been a feature of revenge tragedy to end with such a masque, only to have the masquers turn upon their hosts in a bloody act of vengeance. (A masque had historically been used in the reign of King Richard II to kidnap Thomas of Woodstock, who was then murdered.) The play-within-the-play at the end of *The Spanish Tragedy,* the masques in Marston's *Antonio's Revenge* and *The Malcontent,* the double masque in *The Revenger's Tragedy* would have been known to the King's Men as well as to Webster. Excitement, surprise, the dropping of disguise were features which belonged also to secret revenge.

Webster developed the old rite, which had its own security built in, into a new drama of insecurity and scepticism. Open alternatives are left by him unresolved. His rite is not one of harmony but of disharmony, not of brilliant light but of darkness. As the ghost of the old revenge play has become no more than the active image of a mourner's fancy, so the melancholy of a Prince Hamlet is domiciled not only in the Cardinal, "a melancholy churchman," but in Rosencrantz's successor, Bosola the spy.

At Court, the fable, however slight, must be strongly symbolic; the music, dancing and splendid costumes offered a delicate blend of homage to the King, to the Ambassadors of other kings, to the Court, and to some divine Truth which was being "shadowed" platonically by the action.

The Duchess of Malfi opens with tilting matches and her brother's warning the Duchess to give over her chargeable revels; he characterizes them (as they were often characterized in tragedy) as breeding-places for lust. Her little masquerade with Antonio follows immediately, when she leads through a discussion of accounts and testamentary deposition to the wooing.

Ferdinand's sudden appearance in his sister's bedchamber with his gift of a poniard is a masquerade of the deadliest kind; her own masquerade of dismissing Antonio follows, but he and she cannot resist playing upon their real situation with such quibbles as "H'as done that, alas, you would not think of" and "You may see, gentlemen, what 'tis to serve a prince with body and soul"(3.2. 183–209).

There follows a dumb show of the Duke and Cardinal receiving the news, whilst Delio and Pescara interpret to the audience the sinister mime:

> These are your true pangs of death,
> The pangs of life, that struggle with great statesmen.
>
> (3.3.56–57)

The second dumb show (of the Cardinal's assuming a soldier's habit, and the banishment of the Duchess and Antonio from Ancona) is conducted before a very rich shrine. It leads directly into the scene of the Duchess's capture, and the inverted rites of the prison scenes, whose masque-like character has already been shewn.

It has already been pointed out also that Webster's elegy for Henry, Prince of Wales, who died on the eve of his sister's wedding, provided material for *The Duchess of Malfi*. Laments for the Prince were often bound up with wedding songs for the Princess. This is powerfully reflected in the elegy by a little fable of how Sorrow is masked in the robe of Pleasure. This fancy of ceremony being used for the opposite purpose to its original one may be taken as a clue to the way in which Webster, in his tragedy, is using the masque—the more masterfully, since a blending of "mirth in funeral and dole in marriage" had actually occurred in the winter of 1612–13.

Webster's *A Monumental Column*, registered on Christmas Day 1612, within six weeks of the Prince's death, was bound up with other elegies by Cyril Tourneur and Thomas Heywood. The religious note is here sounded clearly and unequivocally. Webster was to remember Prince Henry again ten years later, in his very latest production.

Theories that Henry and his sister had often been reflected in the drama have been put forward of recent years. In this play Webster transmuted the sorrow that rose from the failure of national hope in one who, like the Duchess, "died young," into a sorrow that could not be defined, that resisted comfort. He took his elegiac fable from an old play, *The Cobbler's Prophecy* by Robert Wilson, which means perhaps that it was still performed. Pleasure was sent down to earth by Jupiter, but, recalled in thunder, left behind on her ascent her "eye-seeded robe" (a common dress in masques). Next comes Sorrow—who bears a likeness to Bosola:

> Sorrow that long had liv'd in banishment,
> Tugg'd at the oar in galleys, and had spent
> Both money and herself in court delays
> And sadly number'd many of her days
> By a prison Kalendar.
>
> (ll. 162–66)

Finding the robe, her face painted by an old Court lady, Sorrow is disguised and courted by great statesmen, to whom she gives

> intelligence that let them see
> Themselves and fortune in false perspectives.
>
> (ll. 184–85)

And "since this cursed mask, which to our cost / Lasts day and night" any Pleasure is false; as Robert Wilson had said, " 'Tis pain that masks disguised in Pleasure's weed."

Pain is the "disguised" feeling that unites the unsympathetic twins, Ferdinand and his sister; pain, disguised by Bosola under many maskings, emerges at last as welcome:

> It may be pain, but no harm to me, to die
> In so good a quarrel.
>
> (5.5.99–100)

And Antonio had suggested at parting from the Duchess (3.5.61–65) that they are like some delicate, fine instrument, being taken to pieces to be mended; here he echoes the elegy:

> Like a dial broke in wheel or screw
> That's ta'en in pieces to be made go true.
> (*A Monumental Column,* ll. 241–42)

This hope he cannot sustain; his dying words are

> Pleasure of life, what is 't? only the good hours
> Of an ague.
>
> (5.4.67–68)

If an overarching fable were to be sought for the whole play, it could be a masque of Good Fame. This was a favourite figure in masques, and the central one in Ben Jonson's *Masque of Queens*; good fame is immortality. Antonio pledges care of her good fame to his Duchess, Ferdinand tells her that reputation, once lost, is lost for ever. The very curious fable that she tells Bosola on her capture implies that good fame cannot be discerned till death; only a complete life may be measured, when those who seem to have few claims may be found to have most. Bosola himself had earlier promised the Duchess good fame through the poets who heard of her story; and this was indeed the way in which it was kept alive.

The Cardinal's good fame is destroyed at his death. At the very last, the faithful Delio brings on the eldest son of Antonio and the Duchess, hoping to instate him in "his mother's right." This was not the Duchy of Amalfi but her personal dowry; yet such an action would involve the recognition of a legitimate marriage, for a bastard could not inherit anything. It is Delio who closes the play on the simplest of major harmonies:

> Integrity of life is fame's best friend,
> Which nobly, beyond death shall crown the end.

From the complexities that negate it, this proverbial flourish may be rescued if it is applied to the play itself. It is in fact Webster asking for his reward, his applause. "Crown the end." On this occasion he received it.

Continuity in the Art of Dying: *The Duchess of Malfi*

Bettie Anne Doebler

The tilt of Jacobean tragic symbolism towards the melancholy undergoes an ironic balancing towards comfort as Webster uses elements from the old *ars moriendi* tradition to structure the death scenes in act 4 of the *Duchess of Malfi*. By 1612 or shortly afterwards when the *Duchess* was written, Webster employed his inventive dramatic imagination to refurbish the worn garments of the popular *ars* instruction so that they virtually glitter with poetic paradox. The art of dying well, at the heart of medieval and Renaissance iconography of death, had shifted in the last ten years of the sixteenth century from a major focus on its reassuring tragicomic ending to an increasing emphasis upon one of the temptations. Literature of the nineties reflects a growing fear of falling victim to the temptation of despair. In spite, however, of such a seeming shift towards darkness, many writers, devotional and literary, continued in the first quarter of the seventeenth century to explore paradoxical reconciliations of hope and despair within the tragic frame.

Webster, known for his interest in death scenes, orchestrates a fearful comfort through the murder of the Duchess by Bosola. Such a macabre tour de force transcends all earlier questions of the Duchess's guilt or innocence in what Clifford Leech has called the "long ecstasy of pain" in act 4. It is Webster's genius that he creates this transcendence through an integration of symbolism from the ars tradition with his own poetic voice.

The sophistication of Webster's dramatic poetry does not therefore

From *Comparative Drama* 14, no. 3 (Fall 1980). © 1980 by Clifford Davidson, C. J. Gianakaris, and John H. Stroupe.

spring forth miraculously without roots. The symbolism of the ars moriendi in varying degrees of literalism and displacement is integral, for example, to many earlier plays of Shakespeare. The conscience scene the night before the death of Richard III on the eve of the battle of Bosworth Field only slightly displaces the old temptation to despair. In the original woodcut, the demon parades before the eyes of the *moriens* all the past sins of a lifetime. In keeping with the popular association of despair with suicide, the demon also offers a knife, and the Latin banderolle translates "Kill thyself." In Shakespeare the ghosts of those Richard has murdered become an analogous parade of sins, almost liturgically ordered in their refrain: "Despair and die." In the major tragedies the use of the *ars* is less explicitly developed, but *Othello, Lear, Macbeth,* and *Hamlet* incorporate many assumptions and images that are (if not directly from the main line of the tradition) from the rich storehouse of death iconography that formed part of the elaborate ritual by which European persons of that age distanced the terrifying fear of spiritual death.

It is no surprise that these and other death scenes of Elizabethan and Jacobean tragedy have rich associations with the old ars tradition. The particular iconography of death with which I am concerned in the European Northern Renaissance stretches from the years of the great plagues, before the first elaboration of the ars series about 1450, to the end of the seventeenth century, as one may see from Romeyn de Hooghe's detailed baroque version of the death of the Christian. Caxton published an unillustrated translation of the popular medieval text of the ars moriendi in 1490, and the eleven woodcuts of the series with the five temptations, the five inspirations, and the happy death were frequently reproduced on the continent throughout the sixteenth century. In England perhaps they were seen most often as single illustrations. Examples appeared in continental books and in popular English devotional books. They surfaced also in tomb art and as stained-glass windows in churches. Some of the single motifs of death associated with the conflation of the ars moriendi and the dance of death were engraved on plate, armor, and jewelry. The ubiquitous skull of the *momento mori,* in addition to its appearance in numerous paintings as a reminder of the fragility of life, took the form of one rare gold watch signed by Jan Heyder and also of a silver one as late as 1650. In addition to his famous Dance of Death series, the painter Holbein, after moving to England during the early sixteenth century, had made at least three designs for jewelry depicting the Last Judgment.

Within the ars moriendi tradition the deathbed became the greatest moment for testing these complex issues—partly because it came at the end of a lifetime of living well or not well, partly because it represented that last opportunity for tuning the soul—a tuning upon which hung an eternity, as Donne makes vivid for us in his "Hymne to God my God, in my sicknesse." The old folklore surrounding the tradition had it that the devil was making a last mighty attempt to capture the soul on its deathbed, at the moment when it was weakest. But the tradition also dramatized one's guardian angel as an opposition to demons—God's mercy against diabolical forces of temptation. Later in the tradition, especially in the latter half of the sixteenth century, friends of the dying were urged to function in the manner of the guardian angel. The heroism of virtue was softened by the suggestion of a shared dependence upon the communion of love.

The theology at the heart of the deathbed ritual as it developed in the devotional literature with such writers as Erasmus and the Protestant William Perkins was one that balanced fear and promise. The opposition between virtue and vice, or the old structure of the *psychomachia,* was in the background. On the one hand, the warning to prepare for the demonic onslaught was constant; on the other, the promise of mercy had always been built into the symbolism. Even though the visual and verbal iconography did not always show the presence of both sides of the theological equation, fear and comfort, hell and heaven, justice and mercy, the reconciliation of those opposites had been built into two hundred years of visual and verbal expressions. Samuel Chew's *The Virtues Reconciled* makes the point that the concept of justice was always balanced by mercy both in visual presentations and in literary documents of the fifteenth and sixteenth centuries. How could it be otherwise as long as the consideration of such virtues was focused upon the salvation of the soul? That the struggle suggests in many iconographic instances a kind of equally balanced choice seems obvious, but in many instances, certainly in the series of the ars moriendi, one must note that the balance is tipped towards mercy. Tragicomedy is the Christian structure. The final scene of dying in the fifteenth-century series shows the triumph of the guardian angel, supported by Christ and the Communion of Saints, as the soul of the dying one is taken up into heaven.

Especially in the dramatic and literary tradition of the late fifteenth and sixteenth centuries, the simple balancing of the five temptations and the five inspirations of the ars series seems, however, to have shifted, especially as popular concern often focused on the bad death. In death scenes I have examined, the temptations against faith, to impatience, to vainglory, and even to avarice (or too deep an attachment to the world) seem all to have been relegated to a less dangerous position than that of the temptation to despair. It seems clear that the temptation against faith had become conflated with the temptation to despair and that impatience and avarice were seen as temptations that must be dealt with well before that last heroic necessity for struggle. Perhaps, after all, it is part of the same pattern by which Tillyard sees Renaissance literature as simplifying the elaborate medieval symbolism.

In the original woodcut from the ars series the demons tempt to despair by bringing before the eyes of the moriens all his past sins. Suicide came to be the feared response to such a state of mind, as Susan Snyder indicated in her definitive article "The Left Hand of God" (*Studies in The Renaissance* 12 (1965): 18–59). The inspiration of the angel then suggests the double remedy against such destructive remorse. Both the visual and the verbal advice was this: "You who think of yourself as a sinner unworthy of the mercy of God can look for comfort to St. Peter, who denied the Lord three times; to St. Paul, who had to be struck down blind on the road to Damascus for persecuting the Lord's people; to St. Mary Magdalen, called from a life of sinful lust to devotion." Secondly, the figure of the thief on the cross is prominent in the woodcut, with the manna of grace raining from heaven as an instance of last-minute forgiveness. In the literature, the moriens is instructed always to keep the image of Christ on the cross also before his eyes. In fact, the crucifix placed over the eyes was early considered an efficacious protection against demonic images.

In dramatic examples in the sixteenth century, despair appears in many variations, but the basic opposition between despair and faith in the mercy of God remains essential for understanding the way of the salvation of the soul. The rope or halter appears more frequently as part of the iconography than the knife, partly because of the late identification of Judas with despair. In both George Wapull's morality play, *The Tyde Tarryeth No Man,* and also in *Mundus et Infans* Despair is ultimately routed by reminders of God's mercy. A similar image of Desperation as a woman who has hanged herself appears occasionally in the emblem books. Allegory, of course, in the late sixteenth century provides another canvas for variation, and the most profound treatment of the subject appears in Spenser's Despair Canto, where the dread hermit speaks those words of reasonable cynicism that threaten to entrap us all.

Obviously the predominance of the Despair image as the mighty opposite to trust in the mercy of God is linked more closely to images of a bad death than to those of a good one. For that reason it may be helpful to begin there in establishing the relationship to Jacobean tragedy. It seems clear, for example, that Macbeth died in heroic despair. The image of his life throughout the play is bodied forth as a life of tragic mistakes and agonizing punishment. The imagery is apocalyptic in its suggestion of an inner experience of hell as the consequence of evil choice. Lady Macbeth is the even more typical figure of despair in the play. The audience knows that she may have died by her own hand, the suicidal epitome of the sin. From his response to her death Macbeth shows his loss of a sense of connection with God's mercy; indeed, throughout the play he serves increasingly and descendingly the gods of his own ambition and necessity. The justly famous soliloquy by which he uses his wife's death to comment upon reality and life as "walking shadow," the frail light that shows us the path to "dusty death," is both magnificent poetry and the essence of bad moral philosophy. From the point of view of the ars moriendi tradition such attitudes reveal a lack of response to the created world and therefore a dangerous state of mind in its response to its Creator. The overlay of heroic convention at the end does little to transform Macbeth's despair, though superficially he dies bravely.

Lear's death, however, is more subtly presented than Macbeth's, and is more interesting to explore partly because it appears in the most profound of Shakespeare's tragedies. Its greatness lies partially in Lear's role as that of a king who learned to be wise through tragic error and madness, for he is not a stereotyped Renaissance figure of ambition such as Macbeth. The conventions of the ars are not obviously present in *Lear;* it is nothing like the virtual adaptation of the medieval temptation to despair with which Richard III is beset the night before the battle of Bosworth Field. Nevertheless, Lear's death is so agonizingly close to despair that we need to look at it again in relation to some of the assumptions of the ars tradition in order to arrive at a reasoned conclusion concerning the play.

The central critical argument about Shakespeare's *King Lear* seems to be whether the tragedy is ultimately one of despair or one of hope. An influential modern scholar, William Elton, in his book *King Lear and the Gods,* comes down at last, after a good deal of sophisticated qualification, on the side of pessimism. It is even more fashionable among Shakespearean critics today to insist that it all ends in ambiguity, that the rich and comprehensive picture of reality in Shakespeare's art denies conclusion or closure.

The latter is on one level an unanswerable argument. Literature never allows for final or absolute answers; literary form itself is always to some extent ambiguous as well as ambivalent in its treatment of reality. At the same time, however, dramatic structure as well as poetic language itself is historical, and it seems to me a modern fallacy to assume that Shakespeare created his plays outside a framework of moral judgment. The power and pervasiveness of the religious perspective was still far too deeply ingrained in early seventeenth-century poetic structure to allow for such a possibility. The still vital image of the Last Judgment which we see in the imagination of such a worldly poet as Ralegh, among others, argues the corresponding place of moral judgment in this life.

Against this devotional and dramatic background Webster creates his own pattern of poetic structure. Specific allusions to the tradition and language of the ars become iconic structure in *The Duchess of Malfi*. Even here we do not see the exact parody of ars conventions as in Falstaff's death reported in *Henry V* (2.3.), but the rich texture of allusion suggests that the commonplaces are immediately apprehensible by the audience as they emerge from the imagery. Despising the world, living a good life, meditating on death as a way of self-knowledge, coming to an existential experience of the necessity for mercy through facing one's sin, and finally overcoming despair through throwing oneself on the mercy of God—all these devotional assumptions are a major part of the structure of understanding demanded early by the dramatic action of Lear, but when we turn to Webster's *Duchess of Malfi* we find such assumptions in more obvious expressive forms. The symbolic language of the play is larded in particular with allusions to the devotional tradition. More specifically, the death of the Duchess is played against brilliant allusions to the language of the ars moriendi. The two scenes of her dying would normally bring to the audience all kinds of visual reminders of the woodcut series and the symbolism developed for them.

The play echoes Counter-Reformation techniques for revitalizing the conventional theological ideas and placing them within a meditative context that moves the affections. Instead of traditional assumptions remaining in the background or being subsumed as they are in *Lear,* they confront the audience vividly and immediately. Webster makes them part of the texture of the play's imagery, often shocking an audience into awareness of the sensuous reality of what is going on dramatically. He creates in the death of the Duchess a kind of composition of place that drew his audience into a meditation on death—not only hers but theirs. Her death is doubly powerful in arousing the emotions because it is a violent killing, an unjust murder of a virtuous and heroic figure.

The scene is actually restrained, however (difficult as it may be to talk of restraint in terms of Webster's heightened style), by the references to the ars moriendi tradition. If we remember the context of comfort of the tradition, as an audience we are in a sense reassured about the end of her suffering. We are shown her virtue almost isolated in the midst of the political and personal corruption that makes up much of the texture of the play. Where there was a balance between good and evil figures in *Lear,* the Duchess seems terribly alone in a corrupt world except for the powerless Antonio. Traditional symbolism points outside the play towards a heavenly justice in contrast to the vicious and worldly injustice she suffers from her brothers with their hearts that are hollow graves.

Although the actual murder occurs in scene 2 of act 4, scene 1 leads up to it in an important way. In fact, scene 1 is a displaced enactment of the temptation to despair performed by the demonic and melancholy Bosola on behalf of the satanic Ferdinand. Instead of being shown her own past sins, however, she is first given a dead man's hand and then shown the waxen figures of her husband Antonio and their children, all appearing as if they are dead. From Ferdinand's point of view, of course, these are her sins. Her response is one of despair, the very response intended by Ferdinand. Her longing for death is expressed so piteously, however, that even Bosola is moved. Though she does not kill herself, she says she is "full of daggers." Her curses upon the stars and the seasons in response to a servant's conventional wish for her long life ends in a curse upon her brothers:

> Let Heaven a little while cease crowning martyrs
> To punish them.
> Go howl them this and say, I long to bleed.
> *It is some mercy when men kill with speed.*
>
> (4.1.107–10)

Bosola insists to Ferdinand that when he sees her next he will make his business that of "comfort."

It is within that context that the actual murder takes place. Bosola shifts his role in terms of the ars tradition from that of demonic tempter to despair to that of the angel who brings comfort. The irony that he is also the murderer only increases the tragic power of the scene. Before he enters we are shown another glimpse of the Duchess, suffering, but suffering stoically, not yet mad but asking of Cariola whether we shall "know one another / In th' other world" (ll. 18–19). As if the dead hand and spectacle of the figures of Antonio and her children were not enough to drive her to despair, Ferdinand has provided another little variation upon horror. Ostensibly to cheer her melancholy, he sends several kinds of madmen: a lawyer, a secular priest, a doctor, an astrologian, a tailor, an usher, a farmer and a broker. A seventeenth-century audience would have found the variety amusing perhaps with its sense of madness as comic, but the actual language of the individuals, filled with obscenity and demonic imagery, would more importantly create the context of earthly reality as an experience of hell itself around the Duchess.

Bosola enters in the guise of an old man, suggesting the figure of death, saying that he is come to make her tomb. Her response "Thou speak'st as if I lay upon my deathbed" (4.2.117) immediately would bring to the mind of the Renaissance audience the frequent deathbed scenes of the period. When the Duchess asks Bosola who she is and he answers, "Thou art a box of worm-seed" (4.2.124), we know he is beginning the familiar *contemptus mundi* theme, playing upon the frailty and mortality of the flesh, descrying the body as the prison-house of the soul. When reminded that she is after all the *Duchess,* he presents a meditation upon the vanities of such worldly position. The Jacobean audience, familiar with both the tradition of melancholy and the commonplaces of the ars, would have been aware of the effect of such meditation: to detach the one about to die from the last vestiges of *avarice,* not in this broad sense an inordinate desire for wealth and possessions, as Bosch in *The Death of the Miser* portrays it, but any last desire to cling to the transitory. The proper mood for death included not only the assurance that one's sins could be forgiven, but also the "ripeness" and "readiness" we recall in Shakespeare. One must not despair of mercy and therefore wish for suicide; paradoxically, one must feel no ties to this world—one must be ready to move into another context, symbolized in the ars woodcuts by the Communion of Saints portrayed behind the bed. One must be ready to leave behind even friends and family.

The latter attachments are little problem for the Duchess since she believes her husband to be dead. Bosola moves from the contemptus mundi through a witty dialogue with the Duchess into the next phase of the ritual. Executioners enter with the coffin, cords for strangling, and a bell. He rings the bell and recites a poem or song intoning her doom:

> Don clean linen, bathe your feet,
> And (the foul fiend more to check)
> A crucifix let bless your neck.
> (4.2.191–93)

Here again the details of the ars are alluded to, specifically the cross as amulet against the final tricks of the devil. Bosola claims at this juncture to be the bell-man and proceeds to separate Cariola from her mistress. The way of death by strangling is said by Bosola to be particularly terrifying. It may after all suggest the death of despair by one's own hand, but the Duchess more or less rules out that association by her courageous denial that the manner of death is important. Her heroism, in fact, is used to reassure the audience of her heavenly end:

> Pull, and pull strongly, for your able strength
> Must pull down heaven upon me.
>
> (4.2.230–31)

Almost immediately, however, she indicates that her stoical heroism includes Christian humility:

> Yet stay; heaven-gates are not so highly arch'd
> As princes' palaces: they that enter there
> Must go upon their knees.—(Kneels.)
>
> (4.2.232–34)

Bosola strangles her and, one feels, the audience of the time might well have imagined the presence of an angel taking her soul up into heaven. It is not until later in the scene that Webster takes a leaf from *Othello* and *Lear* and has Bosola see her stir with the heaven in her eye which would take him "up to mercy" (l. 349). The brief respite gives him a chance to tell the truth about Antonio, but she, of course, dies with "mercy" on her lips.

Even so brief a critical summary of the Duchess's murder marks elements used liberally from the ars moriendi tradition. The symbols and assumptions are built into the text; they are the bones of the dramatic action. Bosola in the first scene is a demonic instrument; in scene 2 the intensity of the irony is heightened by the way in which he as murderer largely shifts his demonic role to that of angel of comfort. The Duchess performs in the ritual as one dying the best of deaths. She is not afraid of death, "Knowing to meet such excellent company / In th' other world" (4.2.207–8). Her last words to Cariola are requests to give her little boy syrup for his cold and to hear the bedtime prayers of her daughter. Her behavior is so stoically brave and true that Bosola by the scene's end is brought to genuine tears of contrition, and the audience with him must surely have been convinced that Webster's attitude toward the Duchess was one of deep admiration.

What does the study of such conventions add to the reader's experience of the *Duchess of Malfi*? Much more than it could add to Shakespeare's tragedies. It is difficult to think of anything external adding substantially to the experience of *Lear*. One might well feel in a measure with the so-called New Critics that *Lear* is great enough in the richness of its own language to escape reference to contexts. Even its language, however, is richest as understood within the complex of historical attitudes from which it came. The affirmation of mercy that links Cordelia and Edgar to the ars tradition helps support the positive statement of the play that is so often ignored or lost in the towering agonies of the tragic experience. *The Duchess of Malfi* gains more obviously and perhaps less profoundly from seeing it within the context of the appropriate tradition.

From an historical perspective both plays are important in assessing the tenuous relationship in the early seventeenth century between despair of one's future salvation and trust in the mercy of God, a paradox that works backwards upon our attitudes towards this life. In the devotional tradition the necessity to face the quality of one's life is seen as part of one's necessary path to humility; at the same time the assurance of mercy must allow for the full experience of contrition and reconciliation. The trust that ultimately one shall rest in God's hand is, according to the devotional writers, the end of a life of daily dying—that is to say, of assessing and savoring life in terms of limit. In the final scene of life itself, be it tragic or otherwise, the seventeenth-century audience saw such patterns. For the mind of the time the moment of death was existentially vital; the structures of the ars moriendi provided rich support for hope of favorable judgment and therefore confidence in the very quality of life itself. Such an art of devotion and drama kept the essential balance between fear and love and spoke to the possibilities inherent in this life.

Tragedy, which for the Elizabethans and Jacobeans ended in so much death, had a great deal to say about hopes for this life. *Lear* affirms the hard truth that whatever the cost love is worth it, and that order will be restored. The *Duchess* is more doubtful. The ars assumptions and images are used mainly to establish the melancholy sense of a dying and corrupt polis, its ministers those of despair and its comfort from hell. However splendid the heroism of the Duchess, it stands upon a somewhat flimsy romantic erot-icism. Even her Christian dying provides the predominantly conventional hope for a future justice, and in spite of Bosola's conversion to a minister of revenge, we are left doubting that the world can change. In Webster the ars, though still a convention of comfort, has become more other-worldly and less vital, as if the essential balance of fear and hope were in danger. It still softens the tone towards comfort. In the devotional tradition and in the tradition of poetry it survives at least through Milton, but in drama there is earlier to be seen a weakening of the essential moral connection between this life and the next. The power of transcendent reality to affect a person's life is in the *Duchess* an emerging question.

"To Behold My Tragedy": Tragedy and Anti-tragedy in *The Duchess of Malfi*

Jacqueline Pearson

The failure of *The White Devil* in 1612 seems to have caused Webster to reevaluate his own view of tragedy and its relationship with other dramatic genres. Certain methods of construction remain, clashing tones, the use of satirical commentary and ironic repetition, but differences between the plays are perhaps more striking. *The Duchess of Malfi* makes little use of the moral redefinitions of *The White Devil*: good and evil are more clearly meaningful, and ambiguity less an expression of the real nature of the world than an evasion. The Duchess is a far less ambiguous heroine than Vittoria, a good woman who is forced by the threatening society around her into an equivocal situation, hiding behind "masks and curtains" (3.2.159) when she would prefer frank and open demonstrations of feeling, expressing herself "in riddles and in dreams" (1.1.446) when she would prefer to speak clearly and unambiguously. *The White Devil* is centred on ambiguous characters, the later play on more obviously tragic figures, a great lady who loves too well and is murdered at the instigation of her brothers. *The White Devil* from the beginning introduces tragicomic incidents, ironic undermining and the modifying use of laughter. The later play seems at least to begin as a tragedy of passion.

However *The Duchess of Malfi* has created problems about structure and unity perhaps even more seriously than *The White Devil* with its ironic repetition and deliberate fragmentation. The first four acts seem to constitute a tragedy of a palpable kind, but Webster allows his heroine to die

From *Tragedy and Tragicomedy in the Plays of John Webster*. © 1980 by Jacqueline Pearson. Barnes & Noble, 1980.

over an act before the end of the play. *The Duchess of Malfi* begins as a tragedy and only in the fifth act confronts tragedy with satire, tragicomedy, and a distorted view of the tragic absolutes. This method of construction causes critics much uncertainty about the unity of the play. William Archer found it "broken-backed," and Ian Scott-Kilvert finds his final act an "anti-climax" which is "fatal to the unity of the play." However I think this is far from our experience of the play in the theatre, and I want to examine the fifth act and its relationship with what has gone before.

The first four acts of *The Duchess of Malfi* form a coherent tragedy. Indeed tragedy seems inevitable from very early. As early as the end of the first act, Cariola defines the play as a tragedy: to her, the Duchess's wooing of her steward seems "a fearful madness" which deserves "pity"(1.1.506). The tragic emotions of fear and pity are already implicit in the action. As the play progresses, the tragic emotions become more pressing and inescapable. In act 4 the Duchess's torment and death are posed as a formal "tragedy" (4.2.8, 36, 288) scripted by Ferdinand, enacted by Bosola, centred on the Duchess, and developing in the Aristotelian combination of "pity" (4.1.88, 90, 95, 138; 4.2.34, 259, 273, 347) and "terror" (4.2.189). Where *The White Devil* uses "tragedy" or "tragic," it usually includes mockery or at least uncertainty of response. The fourth act of *The Duchess of Malfi* uses such words far more simply and seriously.

The tragic centre of the play is menaced by bitter comedy and by images of fiction which the Duchess must oppose with her own tragic consciousness and her acute understanding of the line dividing truth from falsehood. Bosola's disguises, Ferdinand's equivocating vow, his sinister joke with the dead man's hand, the Masque of Madmen, Cariola's desperate attempt to escape death by improvising fictions, the "sad spectacle" (4.1.57) of the dead Antonio and his son, which turns out to be only "feign'd statues" (4.2.351), the "tedious theatre" (4.1.84), the "good actor" playing a "villain's part" (4.1.289–90), all these create a pervasive sense of fiction and unreality which can only be defeated by the Duchess's acceptance of tragedy with her eyes open, "well awake" (4.2.224). Tragedy is surrounded by and tested by unreality and grim comedy. It is also tested by reminders of a happy past which contrasts poignantly with the present horror. The scene . . . is heavy with echoes of the wooing scene. Again, Bosola's view of the Duchess as an "unquiet bedfellow" (4.2.140) is a poignant reminder of Cariola's banter that her mistress is "the sprawling'st bedfellow" (3.2.13). Under attack from black comedy, from fiction, from reminders of past happiness and illusive promises of a happy future, the Duchess must laboriously salvage the tragic absolutes, insisting upon her own identity and her own clear-sightedness.

Although the Duchess preserves the status of a tragic heroine, she has an ambiguous relationship to some of the absolutes which we might expect tragedy to affirm. She chooses not to "pray" (4.1.95) but rather to "curse the stars" (4.1.96), and the world itself into "chaos" (4.1.99). Throughout the play the Duchess has appeared as spokesman for fruitful disorder by rejecting "vain ceremony" (1.1.456), the traditional role of the nobility, and the traditionally passive role of women. She is contrasted with Antonio, whose conventional admiration for "fixed order" (1.1.6) is only abandoned as he dies. Here for a moment the Duchess's acceptance of fruitful disorder almost slips over into the will for general destruction, but finally she dies in humility and "obedience" (4.2.169), kneeling to enter heaven, and insisting upon her own awareness and understanding, "well awake" (4.2.224).

The most extreme manifestation of anti-tragedy and menacing theatricality with which the Duchess is confronted is the Masque of Madmen. This masque not only attacks the Duchess: it also detaches us from the play-world by presenting a distorted version of it. The discordant music, dialogue in which no communication is made, and the ever more extreme vision of physical and spiritual degeneration reflect and comment on the play itself. The masque and its characters provide a grotesque image of the world of the play, and some of the madmen reflect quite accurately some of the play's central characters. The Third Madman clearly recalls the Cardinal, the corrupt sensual churchman. The Fourth, the mad doctor, may reflect Ferdinand, who imagines himself as a physician treating the "intemperate agues" (4.1.142) of the Duchess, who sent her the grim Masque of Madmen as a "cure" (4.2.43), and who finally needs a doctor to treat his own madness. He himself draws the connection for us: "Physicians are like kings" (5.2.66). The Second Madman—perhaps also the one discussed in lines 103 to 105—is perhaps a distorted version of Bosola, who "shows the tombs" (4.2.102) and indulges in misogynistic and scurrilous stories of "the glass-house" (4.2.77; 2.2.7). The Masque of Madmen, as well as presenting an attack on the Duchess by the forces of satire, also genuinely helps to keep her in her right wits by asserting her essential sanity in the face of the grotesque madness of her opponents, Ferdinand, the Cardinal, and Bosola.

This painful confrontation between tragedy and anti-tragedy is further complicated by links drawn between the representatives of the two. Bosola is not only like Antonio: he is also, in this scene, like the Duchess. The Duchess is "like a madman" (4.2.17), and she believes at first that Bosola is "mad too"(4.2.114). She compares her suffering with that of "the tann'd galley-slave" (4.2.28), and we recall that Bosola had served a sentence in the galleys for a murder commissioned by the Cardinal (1.1.71–73). The two are not only enemies but are also almost allies. Bosola's tissue of questions helps the Duchess to arrive at her self-definition, and his pessimism throws into relief her affirmation.

The death of the Duchess, then, is poised as the play's tragic centre, described as a "tragedy," surrounded by "pity" and "terror," fighting off anti-tragedy, and finally leading to a triumphant affirmation of her own identity, "I am Duchess of Malfi still" (4.2.142). The Duchess is both a tragic heroine reaching a tragic affirmation, and the heroine of a tragical comedy, like R. B.'s Virginia, escaping from tragedy into a heavenly afterlife. However this posed tragedy disintegrates into anti-tragedy after the death of the Duchess. Tragedy is parodied in Cariola's high-spirited fight for life. She creates a tissue of fictions, like "I am quick with child" (4.2.254), which Bosola clear-sightedly recognises as fictions. Cariola is driven into subterfuge, into taking shameful ways to avoid shame. Unlike her mistress, she cannot free herself from fiction even as she dies, and the only kind of love and motherhood she can claim for herself exist in fiction only.

It is not just, then, that in act 5 the play moves away from tragedy: the Duchess's hard-won tragic moment is precarious and collapses as soon as she dies, and the return from tragedy is illustrated in several small inversions or parodies of tragedy. If Cariola parodies the tragic actors, Ferdinand parodies the tragic audience. His reaction to the death of his sister is a perversion of the tragic catharsis experienced by the audience. He first denies (4.2.259) and then accepts the validity of tragic "pity" (4.2.273), sees the event as one of "horror" (4.2.311, 314), and interprets the whole as a "tragedy" (4.2.288). However for Ferdinand pity and fear are not purged: they are violently awakened, so that he rushes out "distracted" (4.2.336). This inversion of catharsis also brings Ferdinand to the reverse of a tragic understanding of the situation: he tries to throw all the blame on to Bosola, to imagine a fictional happy ending, and to retreat into obviously false motives and images of fiction.

At this point, with Ferdinand parodying the reactions of tragedy, in another inversion of tragedy the Duchess revives for a moment. It seems momentarily that all that has gone before is only a tragicomedy which wants deaths. For Bosola, this rich confusion of tragedy and tragicomedy poses insoluble problems. Even the tragic emotions are confused, until it seems that "pity would destroy pity" (4.2.347). Where the Duchess faces and accepts the truth of her situation and Ferdinand recoils from it, Bosola is faced with divided loyalties to fact and fiction, and he presents the dying Duchess with a half-real, half-unreal account of Antonio alive and reconciled to her brothers. Bosola's confrontation with tragedy leaves him still prepared to use fictions, and however kindly his motives this deliberate falsehood suggests that Bosola's dependence on fiction and deception is to shape his actions even now that he has rejected "painted honour" (4.2.336). Where Ferdinand retreats from tragedy, Bosola accepts it in modified form, throwing off his disguise. This acceptance, though, is complex and ambiguous. His change of direction is achieved only when he is convinced he has lost his chance for reward, so that it has a strong undercurrent of personal spite. Moreover it is a change in attitude which does not seem much to affect the way he acts, but only the people who are his friends and enemies. To see Bosola's move to the Duchess's side only as a new commitment "to doing what he knows is morally right" or even as "redemption" seems to oversimplify. It is a strange kind of conversion which is only second choice to material advancement, and which produces the same kind of murder and betrayal as his unregenerate self.

Moreover this change in Bosola is not wholly for the good. It expresses itself not only in a discovery of his own "guilty conscience" (4.2.356), but also in a significant dimming of his clear moral insight. Before this he always showed a clear moral understanding even when this was rigidly excluded from his actions. From this point he no longer stands in a special relationship with the audience, he is less self-critical, and we can accept his evaluations less readily. His vow, for instance, to give the body of the Duchess to "some good women" (4.2.372) is made apparently without irony, although he has just participated in the murder of the play's two good women. Bosola, as he himself would have been the first to realise earlier in the play, returns as arrant knave as he set forth, because he carried himself always along with him.

The fourth act of *The Duchess of Malfi*, then, presents a tragedy in which a good woman achieves a tragic self-assertion. This tragic centre, however, emerges from a mass of anti-tragic material: a masque which provides a grotesquely distorted view of the play itself, a parody of the tragic moment as Cariola refuses tragedy and Ferdinand perverts tragic catharsis, and a miniature tragicomedy in which the Duchess briefly revives. The act tries to suggest as richly as possible the variety of human reactions to disaster without compromising the centrality of the Duchess's positive statement. For the strong few there is the possibility of tragedy: for the majority there is only uncertainty, ambiguity, or the rejection of the difficult absolutes of tragedy. There is never any real doubt about the Duchess's courage and her essential innocence: the play's central ambiguities lie rather in the effect of her love and death on those around her. In the final scene the focus shifts from tragedy to inversions and parodies of tragedy, and from the Duchess to Bosola and Antonio. Without the tough integrity of the Duchess, tragedy falls apart into satire, self-deception, despair and madness.

Dorothea Krook sees tragedy as an interlocking sequence of four units, "the act of shame or horror," the "suffering" which this causes, the special "knowledge" generated by this suffering, and the "affirmation or reaffirmation of the dignity of the human spirit" which this new and special knowledge produces (*Elements of Tragedy*). If this is a valid scheme for tragedy, *The Duchess of Malfi* seems to use the tragic framework in a peculiarly sceptical and ironic way. In the fourth act, the death of the Duchess forms a genuine tragic centre. The end of the act, and the fifth act, provide a series of inversions or parodies of the tragic scheme, in which almost all the tragic values are negated. The first three acts present an ambiguous view of the tragic "act of shame or horror": the Duchess's unequal marriage is seen as shameful and horrifying by Ferdinand, though not necessarily by the audience. Act 4 juxtaposes an authentic tragic "knowledge" with knowledge of a more dubious kind. Act 5 ends the play on an ambiguous view of tragic affirmation.

In many ways in style and in imagery act 5 is very different from the play which has gone before. The play has arranged tragedy as the peak, the highest in artistic form and in moral achievement, from which the final act charts a sharp decline. The language itself changes to emphasise this change of quality. The end of act 4 and act 5 itself are full of negatives, "silence" (4.2.5; 5.4.83), "never" (5.5.90), "no" (5.5.108), "not-being" (4.2.301), and especially "nothing" (4.1.138; 4.2.15; 5.2.33, 39, 54, 231, 330, 347; 5.5.59, 79, 118), which echoes through the last act. After the affirmation of the Duchess's life and death the society she leaves behind her is negative and sterile.

Again in the final act the play's images of comedy and tragicomedy become more extreme and grotesque. Julia's wooing of Bosola begins as an enacted tragicomedy in which she threatens him with a pistol, and ends in tragedy in earnest, rather like Flamineo's death in *The White Devil*. The "fatal judgement" (5.2.85) which falls on Ferdinand, the play's leading exponent of satirical comedy, is that he becomes frozen into this one posture, a comic madman afraid of his own shadow. The Cardinal too dies surrounded by laughter, doomed by the fictions which he thought he controlled.

Act 5, then, is deliberately separated from the first four acts by a change in vocabulary and by an increase in pressure from comic and tragicomic incidents. It is also separated by a change in focus on certain characters. We become increasingly distanced from the characters, and it becomes less and less easy to accept what they tell us at face value, until we can view even the last words of the play with critical objectivity. Those characters who have stood as delegates of the audience, Bosola, Antonio and the Duchess have either disappeared from the play or had this special relationship shattered. Antonio especially, who began the play by guiding our judgements, has shrunk in stature since the death of his wife. His character has fallen apart. Bosola has taken over his clear-sighted grasp of character and Delio his stubborn integrity. Only his less attractive characteristics remain, his subconscious wish for disaster, his helpless indecision, poor judgement, desire for "any safety" (5.1.67). His death at least frees him from fear and from his conventional awe of the "fixed order" (1.1.6) of the courtly life, which he never shakes off and which helps to doom him. Like Ferdinand and the Cardinal, he is destroyed by the death of the Duchess.

Despite Webster's deliberate use of contrasting modes in the final scenes, they are nevertheless tightly connected in theme with what has gone before. The final act might have been a second tragedy arising from the Duchess's murder, an "act of shame or horror" which might have driven her murderers to tragic knowledge and affirmation. However in the final act, tragic structures are suggested only to be negated, inverted, or parodied, or are accepted only in a limited sense. Brooding over this series of anti-tragedies is the strongly contrasting presence of the Duchess. In a significant, almost indeed in a literal, sense the dead Duchess haunts the final act, a constant poignant reminder of a better way of living. After what seems her death she revives momentarily, she "haunts" Bosola, perhaps even appearing as he imagines he can see her, "there, there!" (5.2.346). She is heard again in the echo scene, and again perhaps is seen, "a face folded in sorrow" (5.3.45). Of course she is constantly talked about in the last act, and is metaphorically present in the echoes and summaries of the past with which the ending of the play is permeated. When she appears three times after her apparent death it seems as if she and the life force which she represents are proof against death. Her tragic affirmation confronts the sceptical world left behind her, and the tragicomic discords created by this antithesis modify the effect of the final act.

Act 5 contains a rich number of parodies or incomplete versions of tragedy. Deliberately fictional versions of tragedy have replaced the genuine tragedy of the Duchess: the Cardinal's quite baseless story of the ominous haunting of the family by a woman killed by her own kinsmen "for her riches" (5.2.94) is the nearest he can get to understanding tragedy. This fabrication is a parody of the story of the Duchess: we are reminded of

Ferdinand's claim that he had hoped to gain "infinite mass of treasure by her death" (4.2.285). The Cardinal who tries to define tragedy only in these blatantly fictional terms meets an appropriate death. He is the centre of dangerous fiction in this last act, as he uses "fair marble colours" to conceal his "rotten purpose" (5.2.297–98). In order to dispose of the body of Julia safely, he designs an elaborate fiction, and he warns his followers not to disturb it:

> When he's asleep, myself will rise, and feign
> Some of his mad tricks . . .
> And feign myself in danger.
>
> (5.4.14–16)

He is also threatened by black comedy. His courtiers believe that his shouts for help are simply "counterfeiting" (5.5.20), and they imagine how the Cardinal will "laugh" (5.5.33) at them if they mistake his fiction for reality. By his attempt to manipulate fictions the Cardinal dooms himself, and his death provides both an exact judgement upon him and an exact inversion of the tragic process. Suffering is surrounded by comedy, knowledge brings only despair, and instead of affirming his own identity and his human dignity the Cardinal is reduced to "a little point, a kind of nothing" (5.5.79) who only wishes to lose his sense of self and to be "laid by, and never thought of" (5.5.90).

The Cardinal's death forms a clear anti-tragedy in which the precarious tragic moment achieved by the Duchess disintegrates. The death of Ferdinand follows the same pattern, and is also surrounded by fiction and comedy instead of dissipating them in the positives of tragedy. Ferdinand's madness is another opposite of tragic knowledge. Instead of, like the Duchess, asserting his own individuality, he imagines himself a soldier in a battle which turns into a comment on the breakdown of the family. Both Ferdinand and the Cardinal have a momentary flash of self-knowledge, but it allows them no such affirmation as the Duchess's. Ferdinand quotes Giovanni in *The White Devil* to recognise that "Sorrow is held the eldest child of sin" (5.5.55), but he retains little sense of personal identity or personal involvement. His fate seems to him not to be his own fault, but only to be caused by the nature of the world: "Like diamonds, we are cut with our own dust" (5.5.73). The Duchess manages to look to the future as she dies. Ferdinand can only look backwards, and the Cardinal only welcomes oblivion. Their deaths give only negative versions of the Duchess's affirmation.

The Duchess's tragedy is followed by a number of distorted versions of it which become increasingly foreign to the spirit of tragedy. Cariola resists and lies, Julia refuses to evaluate her own life, the Cardinal and Ferdinand invert and parody the achievement of tragic knowledge and affirmation. The death of Antonio is also posed as an anti-tragedy. The scene of the Duchess's murder is carefully prolonged to allow her to make her final affirmation: Antonio is killed casually and accidentally. This painfully ironic scene casts doubts on the whole possibility of just action in a posttragic world. Bosola, who tries to commit himself to "Penitence" (5.2.348), "a most just revenge" (5.2.343), finds himself inescapably trapped in fictions: the murder of Antonio is seen simply as "such a mistake as I have often seen / In a play" (5.5.95–96). Antonio's death allows the murdered man some knowledge and affirmation: at least in the face of death he finds himself able to "appear myself" (5.4.50). However it is of so subdued a kind that it seems a parody of the Duchess's intensity. He achieves a limited kind of self-definition, but it is a weary kind which consists so largely in regret for his past deeds and the admission that throughout the play his judgement has been faulty. At the beginning of the play he praised the "fixed order" (1.1.6) of the French court. Now he dies with a profound distrust of the ambiguous "order" imposed by great men, wishing that his son should "fly the courts of princes" (5.4.72). Tragedy is replaced by horrifying accident and a disturbing pessimism.

Cariola, Julia, Ferdinand, the Cardinal and Antonio is each the centre of a tiny anti-tragedy in which the values of the Duchess cannot be maintained but are inverted or distorted. The final act, though, centres on Bosola, and his anti-tragedy is the most complex of all. From the beginning of the play, of course, Bosola has been an ambiguous character: "very valiant" but poisoned by "want of action" (1.1.76, 80), he "would look up to heaven" but the devil stands in his light (2.1.94–95). This ambiguity is increased rather than resolved in the final act. Like the Cardinal Bosola becomes enmeshed in fictions, despite his newly good intentions. He uses fiction with the Cardinal and Julia, but also, and this is a new development, with himself. He claims "Penitence" (5.2.348) and uncritically claims to be taking part in a "most just revenge" (5.2.343), apparently without recognising the irony of revenging a crime which he has himself committed. This is underlined by the ironic divergence between his intention of joining with Antonio and his accidental murder of his would-be ally.

In the final act the included incidents move further from the paradoxical calm of formal tragedy. Antonio's death is casual, ironic and muddled; Ferdinand and the Cardinal are destroyed by fiction and comedy. Finally the scene reaches the farthest stage from tragedy in the death of Bosola. Flamineo recognised some "goodness" (*The White Devil* 5.6.269) in his death, the last of the play's many ironic inversions of value terms. Bosola similarly believes it can do him "no harm . . . to die / In so good a quarrel" (5.5.99–100). His play has not, however, like *The White Devil* established this kind of moral inversion as a valid way of summing up a perverse and divided world. Bosola's redefinition of the adjective "good" seems less convincing, an uncritical shifting of responsibility which is the opposite of tragic knowledge. This sense of his own rightness is deeply undermined by the accidental murder of Antonio and the casual murder of his servant, by the stress placed on Bosola's grudging sense of being "neglected" (5.5.87) which lingers to the very end of his life, and by images of uncertainty and of fiction, "in a mist" (5.5.94), "in a play" (5.5.96). Bosola's definition of himself as a justified avenger is also cut across by the brutally simple summing up of his career by Malateste, "Thou wretched thing of blood" (5.5.94).

The final irony in this ironic play is the untrustworthy nature of its last words, which we are forced to regard critically and with detachment: the affirmation of the Duchess's death is dissipated in facile pessimism and incomprehension. Flamineo's critical agnosticism in the face of death sums up the whole effect of his agnostic play. Bosola's does not: the affirmative tragic action of the play which precedes undermines his narrow and conventional stoic sentiments. He insists that men are only "dead walls or vaulted graves, / That ruin'd yields no echo" (5.5.97–98). However we are forced to question this reductive view of human life by remembering that we have just heard the Duchess's grave returning an echo in a literal sense. Again, Bosola speaks of the "deep pit of darkness" in which mankind lives, "womanish and fearful" (5.5.101–2). This quotation from Sidney's *Arcadia* seems to have been altered specifically to create ambiguity about the adjective "womanish," when the play's heroine has been anything but "fearful," and has died refusing to see the world as only a "pit of darkness." Bosola's flip pessimism is discredited by our memory of what has gone before: a world that has produced the Duchess and been coloured by her values might seem to be more than simply a pit of darkness. Bosola's two most negative definitions of human life, therefore, are negated by their context, but this ambiguous and indirect affirmation is the only one which the final act of the play has to offer. Finally Bosola urges "worthy minds" not to fear death in the service of "what is just" (5.5.103–4). This final attempt at affirmation, however, is qualified at the last moment by the sudden insight that he himself is not one of these worthy minds whose death will allow tragic affirmation: "Mine is another voyage" (5.5.105).

Bosola's death, like all the other deaths in this final act, provides an ironic inversion of tragedy with ambiguous knowledge and affirmation. The whole scene, too, takes on the shape of these ironic versions of tragedy. Even Delio's last lines, presented to us as a final summary, turn out to be ironically undercut. Delio attempts to redefine greatness and to sum up the play's suggestions that greatness lies not in birth or power but in moral excellence. The play's "great men" (5.5.118) Ferdinand and the Cardinal have lost their identity as completely as footprints melting with melting snow. Men are truly "great" only when they are "lords of truth" (5.5.119). Only "integrity of life," a complete and moral life, leads to immortal "fame" (5.5.120). The Duchess, like the heroine of a tragical comedy, is assured of some kind of immortality because of her intensity and her goodness. However if Webster intended his audience to be aware of the source of his quotation it could only add disquieting ironies to what might seem a conventional summing up. Horace's ode which begins "Integer vitae" (*Odes* 1.22) praises the man of perfect purity and innocence. His goodness protects him even from physical danger, for even the savage wolf will not attack the truly virtuous man. In Webster's play, however, even the Duchess's "integrity of life" cannot protect her, her husband or her children, from Ferdinand the wolf. The play's last lines which seem to offer a "reaffirmation" turn out to be complex and ambiguous, and so does the play's vision of the future. Antonio's son is to become Duke "in's mother's right" (5.5.113), and we might think that this is a restoration of political and moral order. However the real heir is, as Webster clearly points out to us earlier in the play (3.3.69–71), the Duchess's son by her first marriage, and this child of Antonio's who seems poised to reestablish order is the child whose horoscope predicted a "short life" and a "violent death" (2.3.63), and whom Antonio wished to "fly the courts of princes" (5.4.73). Even the play's final restoration of order, then, is profoundly ironic. The Duchess's tragedy is posed at the summit of a descending scale, and the play returns from this height to the confusions, ironies and uncertainties of our real life.

The Duchess of Malfi seems to me not to be broken-backed or confused but to establish a significant relationship between tragedy and other kinds of experience. Comic, satiric and tragicomic elements are posed to define tragedy objectively and to place the tragic affirmation of a heroic individual in the perspective of an antiheroic society. Fletcher's definition of tragicomedy made clear the kind of play he was *not* writing, that which mixed "mirth and killing" and which included both violence and festivity, "laughing together." This is, however, exactly the kind of play that Webster is writing in *The Duchess of Malfi,* where tragic affirmation defeats comedy and satire but is refused by an unheroic society which rejects the tragic values of the Duchess, wilfully misunderstands them, fails to live up to them, or fatally misinterprets them. Tragedy has learned to tell the Whole Truth. *The White Devil* and *The Duchess of Malfi* include miniature tragicomedies and ironically qualify tragedy: after this in his career Webster specialised in formal tragicomedy, with *The Devil's Law-Case* (1617) and *A Cure for a Cuckold* (1625).

Merit and Degree in Webster's
The Duchess of Malfi

John L. Selzer

More has been written on *The Duchess of Malfi* than on almost any other non-Shakespearean tragedy of its time. Yet the major thematic issues within the play remain in dispute: the question of the Duchess's guilt, the motives of Bosola and Ferdinand, and the difficulties posed by the allegedly "anticlimactic" final act still invite contention. While the emotions that the Duchess and her play inspire may be too heated for one more article to cool, I nevertheless believe that a fresh approach to the play—an approach that investigates the conflict between merit and degree—can contribute to a resolution of these issues. Indeed, an assessment of Webster's treatment of the tension between merit and degree not only helps to vindicate the Duchess's actions, to explain the actions of Ferdinand and Bosola, and to justify the play's final act, but it also establishes Webster's play as an unblinking assertion of the primacy of personal worth over inherited position.

The issue of the Duchess's guilt in marrying Antonio has been debated at length. On the one hand, Clifford Leech accuses the Duchess of "overturning a social code; she defies the responsibilities of 'degree' . . . [by] marrying beneath her." Muriel C. Bradbrook agrees: "to marry out of one's class was definitely wrong, being contrary to the teaching of the Church and to the whole conception of 'order' and 'degree.' " James L. Calderwood, while somewhat more sympathetic to the Duchess, nevertheless condemns her marriage because it infringes on the rigidly established social hierarchy, because her act "displays a disrespect for external realities

From *English Literary Renaissance* 11, no. 1 (Winter 1981). © 1981 by English Literary Renaissance.

which is, as the remainder of the play establishes, dangerously naïve." On the other hand, the Duchess has not been without her champions. William Empson, Irving Ribner, Peter Murray, Frank Wadsworth, and others have defended her by showing that Jacobean mores did permit her to marry a social inferior (Empson and Wadsworth), by pointing to her function as a life-force (Ribner and Murray), or by simply contrasting her to her antagonists. But what is perhaps the Duchess's best defense has not been sufficiently explored: the Duchess decides to violate degree not out of weakness or passion or naïveté, but because she wishes—like Webster—to promote in Malfi a new ethic, one rooted in the primacy of worth over degree.

In his dedication to the play, Webster writes to his patrons, "I do not altogether looke up at your Title: The ancien'st Nobility, being but a rellique of time past, and the truest Honor indeede beeing for a man to conferre Honor on himselfe." The same conflict between degree and merit, between "title" and "truest honor," emerges very early in the play itself. In fact, in the first lines of the play we hear Antonio praise the French court because it is motivated more by merit than by degree. For example, in order "to reduce both State, and People / To a fix'd Order," the French ruler "begins at home: Quits first his Royall Pallace / Of flattring Sicophants, of dissolute, / And infamous persons." Moreover, the king is advised by a council of worthies; "Though some oth' Court hold it presumption / To instruct Princes what they ought to doe, / It is a noble duety to informe them / What they ought to fore-see." Thus, while the French king is not opposed to order, he is against order based solely on bloodline. Antonio's description of the French court is so laudatory that it establishes the French court's rule by worth as a norm for the audience. The same scene, however, makes it clear that the rule of the Cardinal and Ferdinand in Malfi, founded purely on degree, violates that norm. As Bosola says, the Cardinal and Ferdinand are "like Plum-trees (that grow crooked over standing-pooles); they are rich, and ore-laden with Fruite, but none but Crowes, Pyes, and Catterpillers feede on them" (1.1.50–54). With such "flattring Panders" in favor at court, there is no place for one whose only claim is merit:

> There are rewards for hawkes, and dogges, when they have done us service; but for a Souldier, that hazards his Limbes in a battaile, nothing . . . is his last Supportation . . . For places in the Court, are but like beds in the hospitall, where this mans head lies at that mans foote, and so lower and lower.
>
> (1.1.59–62; 67–69)

Although Bosola is complaining here of his own lack of preferment, the fact remains that his words and Antonio's help to create a fundamental tension between merit and degree that the rest of the play will develop.

For her part, the Duchess clearly stands on the side of merit; while she never challenges the concept of an ordered society, she does strive to substitute a meritocracy for her kingdom's aristocracy. For example, she approves of the relative indifference toward degree in the French court, where the "Courtiers weare their hats on fore the King" (2.1.121–22): "Why should not we bring up that fashion? / 'Tis ceremony more than duty, that consists / In the remooving of a peece of felt" (2.1.126–28). Similarly, when Ferdinand argues in act 1 that Bosola deserves the provisorship of the horse because of his ability and virtue, the Duchess gives her quick assent. Moreover, Antonio tells us that the Duchess's rule is itself based on merit. "Her dayes are practis'd in such noble vertue, / That sure her nights (nay more her very Sleepes) / Are more in Heaven, then other Ladies Shrifts," he vows, for "All her particular worth growes to this somme: / She staines the time past: lights the time to come"(1.1.205–7; 213–15). The mention of the word "worth" in this final couplet is important, since the word recurs throughout the play: "worth" and "merit" are constantly associated with each other, with the Duchess, and with virtue; degree, on the other hand, is typically associated with false appearances, with evil, and with money.

But it is in her proposal of marriage to Antonio that the Duchess most clearly articulates her understanding that an appreciation of worth, not degree, should rule people's actions. James Calderwood has already convincingly shown that the Duchess's intent in the wooing scene is to divest herself of her role as social better, to discard degree, to establish herself and Antonio as equals. I would add that the Duchess is not simply making a private choice based on "romantic appeal." Rather, she proposes out of a desire to choose on the basis of "worth" a "compleat man" who has indeed "long serv'd vertue" (1.1. 497–504). For his part, Antonio is very conscious of his social station; he makes sure that his love is not mistaken for ambition or for fortune hunting. But the Duchess's love and her espousal of worth over degree resolve his doubts. True, in the wooing scene the Duchess underestimates somewhat her brothers' wrath ("All discord, without this circumference, / Is onely to be pittied, and not fear'd" [1.1.537–38]). True, she also overestimates her own ability to withstand them ("As men in some great battailes / By apprehending danger, have atchiev'd / Almost impossible actions . . . / So I, through frights, and threatnings, will assay / This dangerous venture" [1.1.385–89]). And true, some of Antonio's worth—certainly at least his courage—seems to fade from the very moment he assents to the match. Nevertheless, such miscalculations should not blind us to the Duchess's motives, nor should it detract from the boldness of her vision. She enters the "wildernesse," the as-yet-uncharted paths, of rule by merit knowing full well what she is doing and what the possible consequences from her degree-minded brothers might be. (Several readers have cited Cariola's comment at the end of the wooing scene ["Whether the spirit of greatnes, or of woman / Raigne most in her, I know not, but it shewes / A fearefull madnes"] as evidence that the Duchess has erred morally. However, it seems to me that Cariola hardly qualifies as a moral commentator; for example, her death vividly shows her weakness and establishes her as a contrast to the Duchess's boldness. Her comment is best seen as another indication of her weakness. The comment also reinforces the *importance* of what the Duchess has done, but it establishes no moral fault.)

Perhaps we can appreciate her position even better if we examine the motives of her brothers. Both the Cardinal and Ferdinand are driven by degree. We have already seen that the elitist brothers rule their courts according to their own corrupt whims and populate their courts with the most unworthy sycophants. Moreover, the Cardinal hides behind the trappings of his high office "for forme" (1.1.157), since his greatness is "onely outward" (5.5.56). Beneath his robes he is, of course, the corrupt churchman, the embodiment of the poisoned Bible he carries, a man who "strewes in his way Flatterers, Panders, Intelligencers, Atheists, and a thousand such politicall Monsters" (1.1.161–63)—a man, in short, who is just the opposite of the French king whose rule is held up in act 1 for emulation. Thus, it is not surprising that the Cardinal allies himself with those who would depose the French king (3.3.1–9). Nor is it surprising that he appeals to the Duchess to shun marriage because of her "high blood" (1.1.324). Ferdinand, however, is even more preoccupied than his brother with "high blood." He too opposes the marriage because of his obsessive fear that "our blood / (The royall blood of Arragon and Castile) / Be . . . attaincted" (2.5.30–32) by a man of low birth. In addition, his fascination with blood and even his tendency toward incest are rooted in an obsession with rank: he curses the Duchess's profanation of their common blood through her marriage ("Damne her, that body of hers / While that my blood ran pure in't, was more worth / Than [even her soul]" [4.1.146–48 Implicit in his words is the Renaissance belief that blood was exchanged during sexual intercourse.]); and he is appalled at the thought of her husband—"Antonio! / A slave, that onely smell'd of ynck, and coumpters, / And nev'r in's life, look'd like a Gentleman" (3.3.86–88).

Bosola, too, is caught squarely in the middle of this debate over merit and degree. Rather like Antonio, Bosola is a man whose best instincts put him on the side of merit. When we first see him, Bosola is making a case to the Cardinal for his just "reward" for his "service" in the galleys and on the battlefield (1.1.32–33). His "foule mellancholly" (1.1.77), his malcontented railings, we are told, derive from his lack of such reward. Throughout the play Bosola continues to sue for the deserts his "merrit" has earned (1.1.34), and to condemn, as we have seen, the courtiers who get their places without such merit. At one point, Bosola even articulates the theoretical argument for merit over degree:

> Say you were lineally descended from King Pippin, or he himselfe, what of this? Search the heads of the greatest rivers in the World, you shall finde them but bubles of water: some would thinke the soules of Princes were brought forth by some more weighty cause, then those of meaner persons—they are deceiv'd, there's the same hand to them: The like passions sway them, the same reason, that makes a Vicar goe to Law for a tithe-pig, and undoe his neighbours, makes them spoile a whole Province, and batter downe goodly Cities, with the Cannon.
>
> (2.1.101–9)

Later he makes essentially the same point to the Duchess after she tests him by remarking that Antonio "was basely descended":

> Will you make your selfe a mercinary herald,
> Rather to examine mens pedigrees, then vertues?
> You shall want him,
> For know an honest statesman to a Prince,
> Is like a Cedar, planted by a Spring,
> The Spring bathes the trees roote, the gratefull tree
> Rewards it with his shadow: you have not done so—
> I would rather swim to the Bermoothes on
> Two Politisians' rotten bladders, tide
> Together with an Intelligencers hert-string
> Then depend on so changeable a Princes favor.
>
> (3.2.300–10)

Of course, in this last scene Bosola is playing to the Duchess's prejudices in order to win her trust; but he is also clearly expressing one half of his true self, the half that "rejoyce[s] / That some preferment in the world can yet / Arise from merit" (3.2.327–29).

Unfortunately, however, there is another side to Bosola, the side that cannot shake his age's allegiance to the concept of inherited position. This side of Bosola pays allegiance to the Cardinal and Ferdinand; Bosola's desire to get what he deserves ironically makes him give homage to degree. Although he admires virtue, he nonetheless accepts Ferdinand's hire, so that he "maist arrive / At a higher place by't" (1.1.283–84); the offer of an office wins over his best instincts: "Let good men, for good deeds, covet good fame, / Since place, and riches oft are bribes of shame— / Sometimes the Divell doth preach" (1.1.315–17). Consequently, Bosola at times contradicts his assertions that support merit over degree. For instance, about Antonio's weakness Bosola remarks, "This proclaims your breeding. / Every small thing drawes a base mind to feare" (3.5.64–65); to the Duchess Bosola suggests that she forget her "base, low-fellow . . . , one of no birth" (3.5.140–43).

One of the primary conflicts in *The Duchess of Malfi,* then, is clear: on the one side is the Duchess, motivated by worth, attempting to institute a rule by merit in her kingdom; on the other side are her adversaries, the Cardinal and Ferdinand, the conservative representatives of degree and aristocracy, the spokesmen for rule by blood. And caught in the middle, vacillating, is Bosola. Now let us examine the resolution of this debate in the play's final acts, when the Duchess's commitment to her beliefs resolves Bosola's dilemma and prepares for the final subversion of her brothers and their doctrine of degree.

Even when confronted with the grimmest of tortures, the Duchess never swerves from her belief in merit. In the face of Ferdinand's bold threats in her bedchamber, she responds calmly and simply with an appeal to the common humanity that allows all people to marry, regardless of degree: "Why might not I marry? / I have not gone about, in this, to create / Any new world, or custome" (3.2.127–29). Later, discouraged by indignities and dangers, she longs for escape—not the escape of "position" but the freedom of the natural order, where position does not matter: "The Birdes, that live i'th' field / On the wilde benefit of Nature, live / Happier than we; for they may choose their Mates, / And caroll their sweet pleasures to the Spring" (3.5.26–29). Despite separation from her family and a summons to prison, she still pledges her loyalty to merit; when Bosola objects to Antonio's low birth, she responds, "say that he was borne meane . . . / Man is most happy, when's owne actions / Be arguments, and examples of his Vertue" (3.5.144–46). Then—in an important but often overlooked speech—she tells Bosola the parable of the salmon and the dogfish, a parable that epitomizes her position on merit and degree. The dogfish, proud of his "high state" and desiring "reverence" for his "Dog-ship," berates the lowly salmon, "no eminent Courtier," who responds with the explicit moral of the tale: "Our value can never be truely knowne, / Till in the Fishers basket we be showne . . . / So, to Great men, the Morall may be stretched. / 'Men oft are valued high, when th'are most wretched' " (3.5.161–66). The Duchess's position remains firm: to her, true worth is determined by high moral value (and by the "Fisher" in the afterlife), not by high birth.

But it is the Duchess's own actions—particularly her courage in the face of death in 4.2.—that firmly establish the primary importance of merit in the play, for those actions reveal that the Duchess has earned, not merely inherited, her position and our admiration. Earlier the Duchess had promised Ferdinand that she could "die . . . like a Prince" (3.2.78–79), that is, that she could behave nobly even while dying; now she makes good her boast. Although the news of the apparent deaths of her husband and children momentarily had moved her to despair, in her death scene her dignity and control return. While Ferdinand attempts to drive her mad, while "Th' heaven ore my head, seemes made of molten brasse, / The earth of flaming sulphure, yet I am not mad: / I am acquainted with sad misery, / As the tan'd galley-slave is with his Oare, / Necessity makes me suffer constantly, / And custome makes it easie" (4.2.27–32). That is, even as Ferdinand tests her humanity to the fullest, her strength and integrity are sustained. Even the dance of the madmen and Bosola's famous disquisition on the vanity of human action cannot break her. Despite all the torment and humiliation, she can again assert, "I am the Duchess of Malfi still," an affirmation that her true and unassailable dignity is rooted in inherent worth, not in the external position she has so completely lost. At last the Duchess dies— calmly and selflessly, thinking of others and not her princely self, and entering heaven "upon [her] knees" like any other mortal, since "heaven gates are not so highly arch'd / As Princes pallaces" (4.2.239–41). In Robert Ornstein's words, the Duchess's "self-possession in the face of death is a spiritual victory rather than a glorious defeat": her death is a vindication of the value of action and virtue rather than a mirror of the fall of the mighty.

The nobility of the Duchess's death is not lost on Bosola. Although Ferdinand's financial offers had won Bosola over in acts 2 and 3, now the

Duchess's actions begin to convert Bosola to her position. Bosola's first report to Ferdinand about the Duchess's prison behavior reveals his growing admiration for her and for her values:

> She's sad, as one long used to [imprisonment]: and she seemes
> Rather to welcome the end of misery
> Than shun it: a behaviour so noble,
> As gives a majestie to adversitie:
> You may discerne the shape of lovlinesse
> More perfect, in her teares, then in her smiles.
>
> (4.1.4–9)

It is noble behavior that impresses Bosola; her behavior gives the Duchess "majestie," even despite her reduced position. Next, after witnessing the Duchess's agonized reaction to the feigned murder of her family, Bosola is even moved to aid her: to the Duchess's despairing "I could curse the starres," he reassures her ("Looke you, the Starres shine still" [4.1.115–20]); to Ferdinand's delight in the Duchess's despair (4.1.134), Bosola pleads for mercy:

> 'Faith, end here:
> And go no farther in your cruelty—
> Send her a penetentiall garment, to put on,
> Next to her delicate skinne, and furnish her
> With beades, and prayer bookes.
>
> (4.1.141–45)

In addition, in the roles of bellman and old man ("in [his] owne shape" he can no longer bring himself to torment her), Bosola ministers to the Duchess: he prepares her for death carefully, bringing her "by degrees to mortification" (4.2.179). And finally, in the role of executioner, Bosola releases her from her sorrows through death. Throughout much of act 4, then, Bosola still technically works for Ferdinand, that is, for hire and for degree; but his sympathies have clearly been won by the Duchess.

Then, Ferdinand's refusal to reward his service—a final indication to Bosola of the perfidy of those who believe position justifies any act and another indication to the audience of Ferdinand's attitude to those born without position—at last completes Bosola's transfer from Ferdinand's side to the Duchess's. Now Bosola "stand[s] like one / That long hath ta'ne a sweet, and golden dreame" (4.2.349–50). Angry with himself and at his murder of the Duchess, he realizes that he has been a servant of degree instead of merit: "Though I loath'd the evill, yet I lov'd / You [Ferdinand] that did councell it: and rather sought / To appeare a true servant, then an honest man" (4.2.357–59). Now he calls upon his new mentor, the dead Duchess, to lead him out of the "sencible Hell" he had chosen and into a new commitment to virtue (the Duchess even stirs back to life for a moment as if to reinforce his new direction). Thus in the final wrenching and contrite speech of act 4, Bosola resolves "to doe good," to do something "worth [his] dejection"—namely, to stamp out, as the Duchess's avenger, the evil order of degree epitomized in Ferdinand and the Cardinal.

Hence, far from being "anti-climactic," the actions of act 5 represent the play's final renunciation of degree. For instance, the manner of the deaths of the Cardinal and Ferdinand so contrasts with the Duchess's death that their degree is mocked and her worth is underscored. While the Duchess's virtue composes her for death, the brothers' reliance on degree only initiates a frenzied disorder. After Ferdinand himself assents to her "excellence" (4.2.292) when confronted by her dead body ("What was the meanenes of her match to me" [4.2.301]), he sinks into lycanthropy, an affliction that gives the lie to his pretensions of nobility through blood by linking him with animals. Where the Duchess died with silent dignity, with acts of virtue, Ferdinand acts and howls like a beast; while Ferdinand had hoped to drive the Duchess mad, it is he who actually goes mad. And when Ferdinand boasts that he will be able to bribe his way out of hell, we see both the pitiful desperation to which his rank has led him, and his own understanding that what he has merited is truly what he has won; as Bosola says, "What a fatall judgement / Hath falne upon this Ferdinand!" (5.2.83–84). Similarly, the Cardinal dies in the midst of his characteristic duplicity, alone and separated from his panderers and flatterers; he dies not like the Duchess, not like a prince, but "like a Levoret" (5.5.61), like an animal. He too has finally gotten what he has merited: "Oh Justice," he cries, "I suffer now, for what hath former bin" (5.5.72–73). Bosola's comment seals our understanding that the Cardinal's death represents a triumph for virtue and justice, and a defeat for degree: "I do glory / That thou, which stood'st like a huge Piramid / Begun upon a large, and ample base, / Shalt end in a little point, a kind of nothing." (5.5.95–98). Moreover, Bosola's own death, he knows, confirms the triumph of merit; his death is a "payment" (5.5.93) for his own foul deeds. Bosola dies lamenting only that his own "good nature" was poisoned by "neglect" (5.5.105–7), that is, by his own neglect of virtue and his lack of preferment by the Cardinal and Ferdinand. And the final speech of the play—Delio's establishment of the Duchess's own son as the next ruler—confirms that Webster's play chooses merit over degree. Not only is the child himself a carefully preserved product of the "seedbed of peace," of the union of the Duchess and Antonio, not only is he the living symbol of his "mothers right"; but also "these wretched eminent things"—the brothers—"leave no more fame behind 'em, then should one / Fall in a frost, and leave his print in snow":

> As soone as the sun shines, it ever melts,
> Both forme, and matter: I have ever thought
> Nature doth nothing so great, for great men,
> As when she's pleas'd to make them Lords of truth:
> "Integrity of life, is fames best friend,
> Which noblely (beyond Death) shall crowne the end"
>
> (5.5.138–46)

On this assertion of the primacy of "integrity of life" over "wretched, eminent things," the play ends.

I do not mean to overstate the positive resolution of the conclusion of *The Duchess of Malfi*. After all, if the Cardinal and Ferdinand are vanquished, the Duchess herself is dead as well; so too is Antonio, the victim of a cruel accident that almost justifies the despair in Antonio's and Bosola's final speeches. Nevertheless, it remains true that a very basic conflict in the play is resolved on the Duchess's behalf. For it is not just that the Duchess rejects inherited values and is ruined for that rejection; she also proposes a new order—an order of merit, virtue, "integrity of life"—and in the triumph of that order she is vindicated.

Emblem and Antithesis
in *The Duchess of Malfi*

Catherine Belsey

The tension between realism and abstraction which characterizes much Renaissance drama is strikingly displayed in *The Duchess of Malfi*. Critical discussions of the play's psychological realism, on the one hand, or its moral instruction, on the other, have proved largely unproductive. Though critics have recognized an elusive power in Webster's text, they have reluctantly concluded that it is ultimately flawed—psychologically incoherent or morally anarchic. Meanwhile, however, we are becoming increasingly aware that the qualities of plays like *Tamburlaine,* for instance, or *The Revenger's Tragedy,* are more readily understood in the context of an approach to Renaissance drama which takes account of its patently nonrealist antecedents. *The Duchess of Malfi,* I want to suggest, is a play poised, formally as well as historically, between the emblematic tradition of the medieval stage and the increasing commitment to realism of the post-Restoration theater.

The realist tradition, which becomes dominant in the eighteenth century and culminates in the well-made play of the nineteenth, places a high premium on individual psychological analysis, narrative enigma, and a dramatic structure which facilitates the unfolding of a coherent action. The medieval tradition, by contrast, deals in the much more generalized psychology of representative moral types (in the cycles) or of "Mankind" (in the moralities), and develops a structure which promotes moral understanding in the audience rather than suspense. Realism (in the sense of which I have defined it) invites close audience involvement in the action; the me-

From *Renaissance Drama* n.s. 11 (1981). © 1981 by Northwestern University Press.

dieval tradition distances the audience from the narrative, repeatedly arresting the action for the sake of moral analysis or debate.

Renaissance drama inherits this tradition of analysis and debate, while at the same time moving toward new conventions of verisimilitude and narrative tautness. The realist element has been the subject of extensive critical discussion, of course, but we have paid rather less attention to the continuing use of the medieval techniques of emblem and antithesis to focus the attention of the audience on the solution to the moral questions raised by the play, as opposed to the resolution of the narrative and psychological enigmas it poses. Dieter Mehl has drawn attention to the prominence of the emblematic tradition in Renaissance drama, and I think that we may extend his argument to find evidence of the tradition not only in stage properties and allegorical dumb shows, but in the structural patterns of the plays themselves ("Emblems in English Drama," *Renaissance Drama* 2 (1969), 39–57).

Emblem books use picture and text to propose an *interpretation* of a *concept* (opportunity, constancy), or the *relationship between concepts* (truth and error, wisdom and experience). In this they are the direct heirs of the medieval allegorical tradition. On the medieval stage the spectacle of Mankind flanked by Good and Bad Angels constitutes a "speaking picture" and its interpretation, an emblem of the human condition, divided between good and evil impulses. In this sense emblematic drama employs a mode of representation which is radically different from the realist quest for lifelike imagery.

At the same time, the tradition of debate in the medieval drama—between Cain and Abel, or Noah and Mrs. Noah in the cycles, for instance, or between virtues and vices in the moralities—depends on a pattern of antitheses. The spectators participate actively in the process of moral analysis to the extent that they evaluate the arguments, behavior, and fates of the contrasted figures. At the structural level the pattern of antithesis appears in the introduction of contrasted episodes, or of comic episodes which parody the main action. The conjuring of the clowns in *Doctor Faustus* is descended from the tradition which finds its most elaborate form in *The Second Shepherd's Play*.

Renaissance drama displays a conflict of interest between the new search for the reproduction of outward appearances and the concomitant commitment to narrative form, and the inherited tendency to interpretation and analysis of what seems to lie behind appearances. Glynne Wickham finds in the contemporary disputes over the adequacy of Renaissance staging conventions evidence of "a head-on collision of two fundamentally opposed attitudes to art: the typically medieval contentment with emblematic comment on the significance of the visual world versus a new, scientific questing for the photographic image" (*Early English Stages*). It is my hypothesis that we may find evidence of a similar collision within the structures of the plays themselves, and that the existence of this collision necessitates a critical approach to Renaissance drama which is not content with the discussion of psychological realism or the moral values of the dramatist.

Contradictory structural elements in *The Duchess of Malfi* generate a tension between its realist features—psychological plausibility and narrative sequence—and the formality of its design. Close analysis of the text reveals that the audience is repeatedly invited by the realist surface to expect the unfolding of a situation or the interplay of specific characters, only to find that the actual constantly resolves into abstraction, the characters into figures in a pattern. The imagery, both visual and verbal, often functions in a way that is emblematic rather than realistic, arresting the movement of the plot and placing the emphasis on significance rather than experience. The effect is a play that presents an anatomy of the world rather than a replica of it.

The tension between realism and abstraction informs the construction of the play from the beginning. Act 1 opens with Antonio's account of the "fix'd order" established by the judicious king of France (1.1.4–22). What is remarkable about this speech is that it tells the audience little about Antonio and nothing at all about the situation which provides the plot of the play. This is unusual in the *extent* to which the speech is isolated from the narrative sequence. The openings of Elizabethan tragedies, though they often do much more, normally offer at least some information concerning the ensuing action. The first scene of *King Lear* introduces Lear's intention to divide the kingdom as well as Edmund's bastardy; the opening scene of *Othello* establishes Iago's hatred of the hero. *The Revenger's Tragedy* begins with Vindice's commentary on the court as it passes over the stage, and his subsequent meditation with the skull explains the sources of his impulse to revenge; the opening of *The Changeling* shows Alsemero in love with Beatrice-Joanna and so points toward the central situation of the play. On the other hand, in each of the first three cases the opening scene has the important function of defining not only the relationships between individual characters, but also a state of society within which the ensuing action is intelligible.

Other instances resemble *The Duchess of Malfi* more closely. The opening of *Bussy D'Amboise* functions fairly obviously as a prologue to the theme of courtly corruption and has something of the static and defining quality of Antonio's speech. But it also serves to identify Bussy's own initial position of Stoic virtue, which is immediately threatened by the entry of Monsieur. It is thus not external to the action in quite the same sense as Antonio's description of the French court. The Andrea-Revenge prologue to *The Spanish Tragedy* is outside the central events of the play, but it frames them, giving an account of the preceding action and leading into the main plot.

Antonio's speech, however, brings sharply into focus a mode of construction which is very different from that of the realist tradition. The speech defines an ideal of government which emphasizes by *contrast* the courtly corruption of the world of the play. It forms not only an integral but an important part of the whole: the play refers back to it many times, as I shall suggest. But it works by establishing an external and static model, not by leading into a sequence of events.

The entry of Bosola (l. 22) and of the Cardinal (l. 28) leads us to expect that the world of the play's action will now be introduced. And to some extent this expectation is fulfilled. Bosola is seen to be a recognizable dramatic type, the malcontent, and his opening exchanges with the Cardinal indicate a specific situation: he is neglected and resentful. At this point several possible developments suggest themselves to the audience: a quarrel, an account of the crime which has led Bosola to the galleys, or the employment of Bosola for some specific purpose. Instead the Cardinal gives three brief and noncommittal replies to his complaints and then goes out, leaving Bosola in mid-generalization about the pursuit of honesty (ll. 42–44). Antonio again invites us to expect an account of Bosola's situation: "He hath denied thee some suit?" But Bosola does not answer the question directly. Instead he offers an image of the court:

> He, and his brother, are like plum-trees, that grow crooked over
> standing pools; they are rich, and o'erladen with fruit, but none
> but crows, pies, and caterpillars feed on them.
>
> (ll. 49–52)

The plum trees and the stagnant pools are stationary, their relative positions fixed in an image which functions like an emblem, simultaneously delineating and commenting morally on the world of the play. There is a specific contrast here with Antonio's account of the French court, which is a fountain nourishing the state (l. 12), and which is purged of parasites like those which "feed" on Ferdinand and the Cardinal (ll. 7–9). There follows a series of images, equally vivid and equally emblematic (ll. 52–69), and all amplifying Bosola's analysis of the Italian court. When Bosola leaves the stage at line 69 we have learned no more of the plot than we knew at line 30.

There follows the entry of the court (ll. 82ff.), and by analogy with *Hamlet* or *Lear*, or even *The White Devil*, the audience might now expect the main lines of the action to be drawn up. What they are offered is a quasi-realistic conversation concerning horsemanship, and a series of double entendres at the expense of Castruchio. The episode gives us no significant information at the level of action. Instead it amplifies further Bosola's images of the court. It is idle (ll. 91–92) like the stagnant pools, and it nourishes flattering sycophants like those dismissed by the French king (l. 8).

The figure of Ferdinand is dominant:

> Why do you laugh? Methinks you that are courtiers should be
> my touch-wood, take fire, when I give fire; that is, laugh when
> I laugh, were the subject never so witty.
>
> (ll. 122–25)

This court has none of the reciprocity of France, where the king relies on a council "who dare freely / Inform him the corruption of the times" (ll. 17–18). In contrast to the French court the Italian one is dramatized, not described: action and interaction between figures on the stage replace an account. But at the same time the episode shares something of the static quality of Antonio's description or Bosola's images. It displays and defines: it does not develop.

The entry of the Duchess and the Cardinal (l. 147) provokes not a situation but further description, Antonio's "characters" of the Cardinal, Ferdinand, and the Duchess. Like the Overbury *Characters* these define a series of types: they are in no sense psychological portraits. They make no attempt to account in terms of motive or past experience for the qualities they identify, nor are they offered as a basis for moral or psychological development. In this sense they are analogous to Antonio's opening speech and Bosola's images of the court, and like them they are related to one another by specific antitheses:

> the spring in his face is nothing but the engendering of toads
> (ll. 158–59)

> the law to him
> Is like a foul black cobweb to a spider—
> He makes it his dwelling, and a prison
> To entangle those shall feed him
> (ll. 177–80)

> She stains the time past, lights the time to come.
> (l. 209)

While light radiates from the Duchess, what issues from the Cardinal and Ferdinand is dark, repulsive, and finally deadly. The contrast evokes the antithesis within Antonio's opening speech:

> a prince's court
> Is like a common fountain, whence should flow
> Pure silver drops in general: but if't chance
> Some curs'd example poison't near the head,
> *Death and diseases through the whole land spread.*
>
> (ll. 11–15)

The emblematic fountain radiates purity and life, or death and diseases. Antonio's equally emblematic portraits of the Duchess and her brothers echo these contrasting possibilities, and the rest of the play amplifies the antithesis, juxtaposing the Duchess's world of innocence, reciprocity, and fertility with Ferdinand's sterile darkness, isolation, and death.

These metaphors of spreading and radiating are oddly analogous to Webster's own dramatic technique. After over two hundred lines the play still has no semblance of plot. Commentary has alternated with episodes which fail to develop a situation, leaving the audience with its expectations unfulfilled in terms of events, but with a strong and expanding sense of certain polarities which the text defines in outline and then in detail, in imagery and then in action.

The long-delayed creation of a situation now follows very rapidly. In only eight lines Cariola arranges a meeting between the Duchess and Antonio, and Ferdinand secures the provisorship of the horse for Bosola (ll. 210–18). His appointment of Bosola as intelligencer follows, and the details of the situation begin to emerge: Bosola is to "observe the duchess" (l. 252); she is a young widow (l. 255); Ferdinand "would not have her marry again" (l. 256). The dialogue now has a strong flavor of realism. Bosola's harsh cynicism is expressed in the language and rhythms of ordinary speech:

> Whose throat must I cut?
> (l. 249)

> what's my place?
> The provisorship o'th'horse? say then, my corruption
> Grew out of horse-dung.
>
> (ll. 285–87)

At the same time, however, a curiously archetypal quality in this episode underlies the realism of the surface:

> Take your devils
>
> Which hell calls angels . . .
> . . . should I take these they'd take me to hell.
> (ll. 263–66)

> Thus the devil
> Candies all sins o'er
> (ll. 275–76)

The language recalls the pattern of temptation analyzed allegorically in countless morality plays. Bosola is "lur'd" to Ferdinand (l. 231) and is entangled, through his own desire to "thrive" in the world (l. 261; compare l. 37), in a web of false reasoning, deception, and self-deception which leads to his damnation. The specific hiring of a spy simultaneously evokes the temptation and fall of Mankind, and the episode hovers disturbingly between realism and abstraction. Bosola's closing *sententia* seems to resolve it into abstraction:

> Let good men, for good deeds, covet good fame,
> Since place and riches oft are bribes of shame—
> Sometimes the devil doth preach.
> (ll. 289–91)
> (The devil or the Vice conventionally "preaches"
> in the morality plays.)

The instruction to the Duchess follows logically in terms of the play's action, but this time it is the ritualistic nature of the dialogue which is surprising. The play itself draws attention to the "studied" quality (l. 329) of the patterned, formal, joint monologue of the brothers, which is punctuated by the strikingly more natural interjections of the Duchess: "Will you hear me?" (l. 301); "This is terrible good counsel" (l. 312). At the literal level the episode tells the audience nothing that Ferdinand has not already told Bosola. It fails to resolve the enigma of his motivation, already apparently deliberately created by the play ("Do not you ask the reason," l. 257). Instead it establishes a contrast between the natural behavior of the Duchess and the curiously contrived, "studied" world of the brothers. Subsequently, Ferdinand's motives remain obscure: his examination of the "cause" (4.2.281–87) explains nothing to our satisfaction, and his dying words preserve the enigma—"*Whether we fall by ambition, blood or lust*" (5.5.72). But the polarity established here is amplified in the rest of the play, which consistently aligns the Duchess with the freedom of nature, and Ferdinand and the Cardinal with a world of artifice, embodied in the waxworks, the masque of madmen, and the violent ritual of the divorce. In act 4 the Duchess is "plagu'd in art" (4.1.111) until she becomes like her "picture":

> A deal of life in show, but none in practice;
> Or rather like some reverend monument
> Whose ruins are even pitied.
>
> (4.2.32–34)

The two parts of the comparison taken together ironically evoke her own previous assertion:

> This is flesh, and blood, sir;
> 'Tis not the figure cut in alabaster
> Kneels at my husband's tomb.
>
> (1.1.453–55)

The effect of Webster's technique is to define good and evil by antithesis, at first in broad terms (the fountain and the poison) and then more specifically (domination and reciprocity, radiance and cobwebs, nature and artifice), and at the same time to show through the sequence of events the processes by which evil reduces good to a semblance of itself. Ferdinand's "artifice" envelops the Duchess, reducing her to a lifeless work of art; his darkness progressively reduces her radiance; his mental hell is realized in the tortures of the Duchess and brings her close to despair.

Further detailed analysis of the mode of construction in *The Duchess of Malfi* would, I suggest, reveal that the technique I have described is consistently maintained. The quasi-realistic surface repeatedly dissolves into *sententiae,* meditations, and fables. Not only does the imagery form a network of echoes, antitheses, and amplifications: whole episodes refer to and parody each other. The distribution of the central characters shows more concern with pattern than with any kind of psychological probability. As Antonio is to the Duchess, so the Cardinal is to Ferdinand—cautious, prudent, restrained. They are figures in a design, not character studies. The high points in the action of the play are realized precisely by arresting the action and drawing the audience's attention to a visual tableau: the Duchess unconsciously isolated on the stage, abandoned by Antonio and threatened by Ferdinand (3.2.); the spectacle of the Duchess confronting the spectacle of the waxworks (4.1.). During the dance of the madmen (4.2.) the Duchess does not speak; the emphasis is not on the psychology of her reactions but on the contrast between her solitary stillness and the grotesque caperings which are an image of the tyranny she is "chain'd to endure" (4.2.60). The dumb show of the Cardinal's arming and the divorce (3.4.) distances what in another play would be a cue for passionate individual response. The commentary of the pilgrims bears precisely the same relation to the visual spectacle as the explanation to the picture in an emblem.

> 1ST PILGRIM. What was it with such violence he took
> Off from her finger?
> 2D PILGRIM.   'Twas her wedding ring,
> Which he vow'd shortly he would sacrifice
> To his revenge.
>
> (3.4.36–39)

The key words "violence," "sacrifice," and "revenge" focus attention on the nature of the evil, not on the experience of the characters. The same principle is more sharply evident in the preceding exchange: "But by what justice?" "Sure, I think by none" (3.4. 34). Abstraction repeatedly prevails over actuality, pattern over situation, structure over event.

Instead of tracing further the details of the play's construction, however, I should like to consider more closely the nature and the implications of the patterns which the technique establishes. As I have suggested, the central pattern is one of antitheses whose function is to identify and define. Thus, for instance, Cariola's terrified efforts to escape death emphasize the Duchess's fortitude (4.2.). Julia acts consistently as a foil for the Duchess. Her relationship with the Cardinal forms a (rather slight) subplot which intensifies by contrast the effect of the main plot, drawing attention to the moral distance between Julia's fruitless and distrustful adultery and the Duchess's marriage. Act 2, scene 4, offers a display of reciprocal accusations of inconstancy, which concludes with the Cardinal's extraordinarily ambiguous reassurance ("for my affection to thee, / Lightning moves slow to 't," 2.4.40–41), and Julia's ambivalent response to Delio's overtures. By act 5 the Cardinal is weary of her; Julia betrays him to Bosola; he poisons her. This sequence is in direct contrast to the increasing fertility and reciprocal trust of the Duchess's marriage.

It has long been recognized that Julia's proposition to Bosola parodies the Duchess's proposal to Antonio both in language and action. Gunnar Boklund complains that this episode comes too late to clarify the moral question whether the Duchess's second marriage is innocent or wanton, willful, and base. It seems to me, however, that this is a question raised by twentieth-century criticism anxious to locate the Duchess's tragic flaw, and not by the play itself, which owes nothing to the Aristotelian concept of tragedy. The function of the intrigue between Julia and Bosola is to reenact in caricature the entire life of the Duchess, and not merely her wooing. As a result of her wanton overtures to Bosola, Julia hurries to her ruin (5.2.258) by coming to participate in "a prince's secrets" (l. 260). In doing so she ties a dangerous knot (l. 264): the Cardinal warns her that possession of the secret may cause her death (l. 266). He poisons her, and she dies exclaiming, "I go, / I know not whither" (ll. 288–89). The Duchess's wooing, by contrast, leads to the "sacred Gordian" of her secret marriage which is the cause of her death. She dies certain of heaven. Julia's intrigue is like a negative photograph of the Duchess's marriage, and part of its effect is to "place" the Duchess in the minds of the audience so that the values she represents are reemphasized after her death. The echo scene, which follows this one, achieves a similar effect by positive means, offering Antonio (and possibly the audience) a momentary vision of the Duchess herself (5.3.45).

During the wooing scene (1.1.361–503) Antonio accuses himself of ambition (ll. 412–13) and calls it "madness" (ll. 420ff.). In case the audience should be tempted to any absolute evaluation and judgment, the following scene opens with Castruchio's grotesque version of the same vice and Bosola's instructions on how to satisfy it (2.1.1–20). Earlier in act 1 Bosola has displayed the more serious implications of ambition: in order to "thrive" in the world he knowingly chooses a course which leads to damnation. Thus placed between exemplum and satire, Antonio's "ambition," which leads to faithful marriage, is seen to be artless and transparent, dangerous in the corrupt world of the play, but morally innocent in the sense that, unlike Bosola and Castruchio, Antonio defies the values of that world.

Similarly, the painted Old Lady serves to reinforce the Duchess's purity. Bosola's "meditation" (2.1.45–60) and his sardonic imperative, "you two couple" (2.1.61), reduce humanity to the level of the beasts. The scene follows the declaration of Antonio and the Duchess that their marriage is to emulate the music of the spheres (1.1.481–84). Far from "tainting" the Duchess as Berry suggests, the contrast defines her, and the juxtaposition of the two scenes embraces the paradox of human nature.

This paradox, that human beings may aspire to heaven or sink to the level of the beasts, is among the main implications of the play's pattern of contrasts. The central antithesis in the play is, of course, between the Duchess who, valuing life, is able to die (3.2.71) and the predatory Ferdinand, man as wolf, destroying others. That the play establishes a polarity between the values of life and death, fertility and destruction is widely agreed. What is not, I think, so commonly recognized, is the number of points at which the pattern of the play apparently calls this antithesis into question by establishing parallels between Ferdinand and the Duchess, only to resolve them again into further polarities. The Duchess's dissimulation, her equivocation, her double entendres, her cursing and her "madness" are in a sense *like* Ferdinand's. (That they are twins, of course, invites a director to draw attention in visual terms to the ironic parallels.) At the same time, however, examination of these points of likeness proves in each case to emphasize the moral distance between the Duchess and Ferdinand. The play thus constitutes an exploration of the nature of evil, setting out to discover whether it is synonymous with particular patterns of behavior, and concluding, I believe, that it is not. Just as the form of the play constantly raises expectations that its focal point will be a series of events, only to resolve situation into pattern or abstraction, so the pattern itself draws parallels between Ferdinand and the Duchess, only to resolve them into new contrasts. As the construction of the play undermines its realism, so its thematic pattern undermines Antonio's self-accusation:

> The great are like the base—nay, they are the same—
> When they seek shameful ways, to avoid shame.
>
> (2.3.51–52)

Dissimulation is the characteristic method by which Ferdinand and the Cardinal achieve their aims. Ferdinand "will seem to sleep o'th'bench / Only to entrap offenders" (1.1.174–75); the Cardinal, who would have become pope by bribery "without heaven's knowledge" (1.1.166), would appoint Bosola an intelligencer and "not be seen in't" (1.1.225). Even in his fury Ferdinand determines to "study to seem / The thing I am not" (2.5.62–63), and thereafter he consistently seems generous when he is most dangerous. He tortures the Duchess with waxworks, ingenious counterfeits designed to bring her to a real despair. In P. F. Vernon's view, "the actions of the Duchess and Antonio in the first three acts of the play are as culpable as those of their persecutors. They are up to their ears in secrecy and disguise." But while it is true that the play establishes an analogy in terms of action, it goes to some lengths to make distinctions in terms of causes and consequences. The mode of behavior which is *chosen* by Ferdinand and the Cardinal is *imposed* on the Duchess and Antonio. The text stresses the reluctance with which they dissemble:

> O misery! methinks unjust actions
> Should wear these masks and curtains, and not we
>
> (3.2.158–59)

It also stresses the inadequacy of innocence obliged to dissimulate. The Duchess has succeeded in "plotting" a "politic conveyance" for the midwife (2.1.163–65), but the suddenness of her labor leaves the guileless Antonio helpless, convinced that they are "lost" (2.1.160). It is Delio who suggests how to cover the situation by giving out the information that Bosola's apricots have poisoned the Duchess, and then devises a way to keep the physicians at bay, while Antonio complains, "I am lost in amazement: I know not what to think on't" (2.1.173). In the same way it is Bosola who suggests the feigned pilgrimage. There is considerable irony in the Duchess's assertion that she can thus "wisely" forestall her brothers (3.2.322).

While the dissimulation of Ferdinand and the Cardinal is designed to entrap and destroy, the schemes of the Duchess and Antonio cloak not "unjust actions" but childbirth and the flight from tyranny. The *magnanima menzogna* (3.2.180) of Antonio's dismissal injures no one but Antonio, whom it is designed to protect. In the case of the stolen jewels the Duchess is said to be anxious that her device should give no offense, far less do harm: "She entreats you take't not ill" (2.2.61). The judgment that condemns the Duchess and her brothers as equally culpable is too simple. Webster shows that the great are like the (morally) base only to display that they are far from "the same." Similar behavior springs from antithetical impulses—to protect or to destroy.

Ferdinand "as a tyrant doubles with his words, / And fearfully equivocates" (1.1.443–44). Again the play itself draws attention to the parallel between the Duchess's equivocation and Ferdinand's:

> so we
> Are forc'd to express our violent passions
> In riddles, and in dreams, and leave the path
> Of simple virtue, which was never made
> To seem the thing it is not.
>
> (1.1.444–48)

For Ferdinand language is part of the mist which obscures the true nature of evil. His equivocation is designed to entangle his victims: *"Send Antonio to me; I want his head in a business"* (3.5.28); *"I had rather have his heart than his money"* (3.5.35–36). His offer of the dead hand to the Duchess is a grotesque and cruel caricature of the wooing scene:

> I will leave this ring with you for a love-token;
> And the hand, as sure as the ring; and do not doubt
> But you shall have the heart too; when you need a friend

> Send it to him that ow'd it; you shall see
> Whether he can aid you
>
> (4.1.47–51)

His double entendres are a form of antagonism directed against Castruchio (1.1.105ff.) or offensive to the Duchess (1.1.336–37). The equivocation of the Duchess, by contrast, is designed to communicate with Antonio. It is not an expression of hostility but a means of reestablishing and reinforcing relationship. Its object is first marriage, and later praise, mitigating the dramatic effect of her simulated rage as she dismisses Antonio: "I have got well by you" (3.2.183); "I would have this man be an example to you all" (3.2.189). Her double entendres are similarly transparent and domestic, secret references understood by Antonio and the audience to her secret marriage (2.1.). The mist generated by Ferdinand envelops the Duchess's behavior, but the effect is to emphasise the contrast between them: parallel again resolves into antithesis.

Ferdinand curses the Duchess: "Damn her!" (4.1.121). And the tortures of act 4 are intended as a means of realizing his curse, "To bring her to despair" (4.1.116) and so to damnation. Ferdinand's efforts are finally ineffectual, but he succeeds in creating for the Duchess a world which resembles hell (4.2. 25–26). Ferdinand's curse "places" the Duchess's:

> DUCHESS. I could curse the stars.
> BOSOLA. O fearful!
> DUCHESS. And those three smiling seasons of the year
> Into a Russian winter, nay the world
> To its first chaos.
> BOSOLA. Look you, the stars shine still:—
> DUCHESS. O, but you must
> Remember, my curse hath a great way to go.
>
> (4.1.96–101)

Bosola's mockery and the Duchess's ironic reply draw attention to the inefficacy of this curse. The stars shine still: human beings are powerless to affect their courses; and the Duchess is aware of their remoteness. Unlike Ferdinand's, this is a curse which she can make no attempt to realize. It is an expression of anguish not of a desire to destroy. She compares the stars to tyrants (4.1.103), but she does not curse the tyrants themselves. The result of Ferdinand's attempts to envelop the Duchess in his own evil is to produce patterns of behavior which externally resemble his own, but it is an empty resemblance, the form without the substance.

The play invites a similar consideration of the Duchess's "madness" in conjunction with Ferdinand's. Ferdinand's is indicated in act 2, scene 5 (ll. 2, 46, 66). It is destructive and self-destructive (ll. 63–64), "deform'd," "beastly" (l. 57). It is finally established in the lycanthropy of act 5. The Duchess's "madness" is her marriage (1.1.506), mad only in the terms of the world she lives in. Ferdinand nonetheless offers her the masque of madmen as an emblem of her state (4.1.124–31). Despite the references in the dialogue to madness (4.2.7, 17), the Duchess reiterates that she is not able to escape in this way (ll. 24, 26), and the masque itself creates an antithesis between the silent Duchess and the chattering madmen. Ironically, they function dramatically as transformations not of the Duchess but of Ferdinand. Like Ferdinand, who would damn the Duchess, the First Madman would draw doomsday nearer (4.2.73). He would "set all the world on fire" (4.2.74–75), just as Ferdinand would "have their bodies / Burnt in a coal-pit" (2.5.66–70), and would despatch Bosola

> To feed a fire, as great as my revenge,
> Which ne'er will slack, till it have spent his fuel.
> (4.1.140–41)

The Second Madman sees hell as a glass house "where the devils are continually blowing up women's souls" (4.2.77–78). His vision is a demonic caricature of Ferdinand's readiness to imagine the Duchess "in the shameful act of sin" (2.5.41). His statement that "the law will eat to the bone" (4.2.94–95) recalls the image of Ferdinand using the law "to entangle those shall feed him" (1.1.180). The Third Madman's insistence that "He that drinks but to satisfy nature is damned" (4.2.96–97) functions as a parody of Ferdinand's attitude to the Duchess's natural impulse to marry again. If the Third Madman is referring here to the eucharistic wine, there is an additional parallel with Ferdinand's behavior: the Duchess tells Ferdinand, "You violate a sacrament o'th'church / Shall make you howl in hell for't" (4.1.39–40). The Fourth Madman is a companion to the devil (4.2.107): Ferdinand is the devil's own child (5.4.21). Like Ferdinand, the madmen are condemned to a perpetual hell of the mind, a sleepless world of perverted sexuality and death. It is Ferdinand, and not the Duchess, who finally escapes into madness.

Thus in each case a seeming parallel resolves into a new antithesis. The effect is not simply to extenuate the Duchess's behavior: rather, the play identifies evil itself—not in terms of individual motive or intention but as a concept—by locating it within a pattern, defining it with increasing precision by a series of contrasts. *The Duchess of Malfi* invites the audience to consider evil as a mode of behavior, only to suggest in the end that it is something anterior to this, at once more mysterious and more substantial. Ferdinand's evil denies all reciprocity: "you that are courtiers should be my touch-wood, take fire, when I give fire" (1.1.122–23); "Do not you ask the reason" (1.1.257); "Distrust doth cause us seldom be deceived" (1.1.241). He incorporates the world into himself, feeding on it like a spider (1.1.177–80), a tiger (3.5.86), or a shark (3.5.123–41), or transforms it in his own image, "Rotten, and rotting others" (4.2.320). Both impulses have their origins in an egoism that verges on solipsism:

> He that can compass me, and know my drifts,
> May say he hath put a girdle 'bout the world
> And sounded all her quicksands.
>
> (3.1.84–86)

His object is "a general eclipse" (2.5.79) which will envelop the world in his own darkness, and the recurrent imagery which aligns Ferdinand with the devil draws attention to the parallel between this and the Satanic desire to transform paradise into hell. The play explores, too, the power of evil, challenging the audience to question the extent of its capacity to destroy. Ferdinand murders the Duchess but he cannot damn her. A corrupt world can darken the Duchess's outward behavior but it cannot touch her soul.

These two areas of exploration, the nature of evil and the extent of its power, are finally fused in the climactic antithetical emblems of act 5, Ferdinand as wolf and the Duchess as echo. The grim comedy of Ferdinand's "treatment" shows the Doctor trying to tame him through fear as Ferdinand has tried to frighten the Duchess into obedience. Like Ferdinand, the Doctor fails. Ironically, Ferdinand is "studying the art of patience" (5.2.45), but his concept of the virtue is a travesty of the Duchess's: "To drive six snails before me, from this town to Moscow" (5.2.47–48). The parallel and contrast between Ferdinand and the Duchess is thus kept before us. Ferdinand as wolf embodies all the qualities we have come to associate with him throughout the play: the symbol evokes a world of isolation, darkness, and destruction. In his quest for total "solitariness" (5.2.29), Ferdinand would destroy his own shadow (5.2.31–41). Evil that preys on the world is reduced finally to preying on itself.

The echo scene shows how the Duchess, too, is reduced: the echo is powerless to protect Antonio; it is insubstantial, *"a dead thing"* (5.3.39). The Duchess's grave is appropriately among ancient ruins where good men hoped in vain to outlast the storms of the world (5.3.9–17). Paradoxically, however, though the abbey is in ruins, it evokes a "reverend history," and equally paradoxically the ruined Duchess survives as a light which shows "a face folded in sorrow" (5.3.44–45). Bosola's final pessimism is thus not entirely synonymous with the play's conclusion:

> We are only like dead walls, or vaulted graves,
> That ruin'd, yields no echo
>
> (5.5.97–98)

It is evil which finally destroys itself and seeks to be "laid by, and never thought of" (5.5.90). Innocence survives as an echo, a reverend history, or a momentary light revealing the sorrow which is its inevitable experience in a fallen world.

It is true that the play offers no answer to the problem of how to survive in a corrupt world. Bosola's solution is to submit to its values, and he is finally neglected. The Duchess goes her own way (1.1.321) and is murdered. Service to Ferdinand is deadly, opposition vain. The play suggests no way of reaching the ideal of the French court, cleansed and life-giving.

It is presumably for this reason that Webster has so consistently seemed to critics incoherent, morally anarchic, or nihilistic. In reality, I suggest, the play constitutes a rigorously coherent exploration of the nature of evil in a fallen world, and the coherence is the paradoxical product of its contradictory structure. The values of the play are implicit in the analysis it offers, and in the formality by which it repeatedly distances the audience from imaginative absorption in the plot to challenge examination of its analysis. The tension between realism and abstraction alternately involves the spectators and draws their attention beyond the intensity of the play's action to its anatomy of the world, inviting them to perceive the world as a deep pit of darkness, irradiated by the memory of innocence, Antonio's recollection of the French court, an echo of the Duchess's reverend history.

In an essay of this length it has not been possible to introduce detailed comparisons between Webster and contemporary dramatists at each stage of the argument. My hypothesis is, however, that if *The Duchess of Malfi* is unusual in the period, it is so only in the sharpness with which it displays the effects of the contradictory pressures on Renaissance drama. In Tourneur, for instance, on the one hand, we see the emblematic mode in dominance; in Middleton, on the other hand, the formal patterns are present but are more fully masked by the realist surface. Shakespeare, as always, is a case apart, and here it is perhaps harder for us to perceive the emblematic elements in the plays because of our rich heritage of realist critical analysis. But in Webster, and in *The Duchess of Malfi* in particular, we are able to identify a precise and productive instance of the conflict between the contrary pressures of residual and emerging dramatic conventions.

The Duchess of Malfi: A Case Study in the Literary Representation of Women

Lisa Jardine

The Jacobean drama has regularly attracted the attention of critics for its lively representation of women as strong, manipulative, self-willed, passionate and controlling of dramatic action. This "masculine strength" wins the acclaim of the critic for its authenticity, and for its real insight into woman's character. It is the mark of the superior vision of the Jacobean dramatist: he sees beyond the contemporary stereotypes of meek and grieving womanhood to the "true nature of woman"—to a full-bloodedly warrior-like femaleness to which the Renaissance for the first time gave a voice. And inevitably in the last decade both feminist critics and female actors have been drawn to the leading female roles in the plays of Webster and Middleton by their reputation for "liberatedness." The temptation to adopt these figures as role-models for our own period has proved irresistible. Helen Mirren, interviewed about her highly successful and critically acclaimed performance as the Duchess in Webster's *The Duchess of Malfi* in the 1981 Round House production, attributed her success with the role to the fact that it is "very much a play for today." "It is essentially a feminist play about a woman who is fighting for her autonomy."

The suggestion that the Duchess, Vittoria in Webster's *The White Devil* or Beatrice-Joanna in Middleton's *The Changeling* are faithful portraits of possible womanhood in the early seventeenth century, or even dramatic projections of a kind of female outlook lurking beneath the calm surface of the Jacobean world, is puzzling, and in my view misleading. The rapidly

From *Teaching the Text,* edited by Suzanne Kappeler and Norman Bryson. © 1983 by Lisa Jardine. Routledge & Kegan Paul, 1983.

growing body of information we can gather from nonliterary sources, both of woman's actual position in early modern society and of contemporary attitudes towards her, is striking for the consistent picture it gives of the *absence* of emancipation of women, both at a theoretical and at a practical level. Where, then, do the strong female characters who wheel-and-deal their way through the drama come from? How are they related to their real-life sisters who were, it transpires, increasingly constrained by an ideology of duty and obedience which removed from them the most elementary possibilities for rebellion against traditional serving roles?

In this [essay] I shall be looking at the impression of strength in the Jacobean female hero in one play, John Webster's *The Duchess of Malfi,* and offering tentative answers to these questions. I shall be suggesting that the "psychological insight" of the Jacobean dramatists' representations of women is related to actual seventeenth-century women and their roles in an unexpected way, and one which must give us pause for thought in our wider exploration of the literary representation of women. This is, if you like, a cautionary tale, and a direct challenge to those who suggest that the vision of the well-intentioned dramatist (be he Shakespeare or Webster or Middleton) can transcend the limits of his time and sex in the representation of women.

Let us begin by trying to identify some of the features of female characterisation which lead the critics to refer to them as "strong" in the first place, and as admirable in that strength. Passion, sensuality, courage, intelligence, cunning, ambition are some of the attributes associated with female heroes like Bianca in Middleton's *Women Beware Women,* Beatrice-Joanna in *The Changeling,* Vittoria in Webster's *The White Devil.* All these qualities are at various times shown by the Duchess. They add up to such forcefulness and spirited independence that generations of audiences have been seduced into accepting them as part of a consistent and believable female heroic persona. And it is in the interests of that "believableness," I think, that the critics are led to assert the correspondence between this "strength" of character and emancipated possibilities for individual women of the period. A recent critic writes:

> One of John Webster's most original contributions to English tragedy consisted in his examination of the characteristics which combine to produce a convincing tragic heroine.
> (E. M. Brennan, in her edition of *The Devil's Law-Case*)

But as she pursues this "convincingness" it emerges that the critic views this in a very particular sense; the "convincing tragic heroine" is convincingly (and, the suggestion is, realistically) threatening to men:

While providing a convincing answer to the question, "What did this woman do to merit death?," the tragedy which successfully presents a sympathetic tragic heroine must also be concerned with the question, "Can this woman be trusted?" It is not a matter of one woman being able to trust another . . . but it is a matter of whether one man or many men can trust one particular woman.

"Can this woman be trusted?" is a peculiarly patriarchal question to ask. And indeed, our critic acknowledges this:

> In Webster's major tragedies this point is emphasised by the strange situation of his heroines. Both Vittoria and the Duchess of Malfi move in exclusively masculine worlds; both appear to be cut off from contact with other women; both are virtually isolated from the friendship or companionship of women of their own rank.

The female hero moves in an exclusively masculine stage-world, in which it is the task of the male characters to "read" her. Is she what she appears? "Look to't: be not cunning: / For they whose faces do belie their hearts / Are witches, ere they arrive at twenty years— / Ay: and give the devil suck" (1.1.308–11). Shakespeare's "strong" women find themselves in a similarly male world: Gertrude in *Hamlet* (and her reflection in Ophelia), Desdemona in *Othello* (more manipulated than manipulating), Cleopatra in *Antony and Cleopatra*.

So when the critic tells us that the Jacobean dramatist shows peculiar insight into female character, and even into female psychology, what he or she means is that a convincing portrayal is given *from a distinctively male viewpoint* (even if this is not made explicit by the critic). Another female critic, apparently content that "psychological insight" into female character be *male* insight, writes:

> Middleton's capacity for tragedy is inseparable from his other supreme gift, his discernment of the minds of women; in this no dramatist of the period except Shakespeare is his equal at once for variety and for penetration [sic].
>
> (Una Ellis-Fermor)

The strength of the female protagonist is as seen through male eyes.

It is seen through male eyes, and as such it is dramatically compelling. But the female character traits to which the critics give this enthusiastic support are on inspection morally dubious: cunning, duplicity, sexual rapaciousness, "changeableness," being other than they seem, untrustworthiness and general secretiveness. In *The Duchess of Malfi*, the first entrance of the Duchess is in an atmosphere fraught with explicitly offensive sexual innuendo, in which she is implicated, and which controls our assessment of her character:

> FERDINAND.   You are a widow:
>   You know already what man is, and therefore
>   Let not youth, high promotion, eloquence—
> CARDINAL. No, nor anything without the addition, honour,
>   Sway your high blood.
> FERDINAND.   Marry! they are most luxurious
>   [lustful]
>   Will wed twice.
>   · · · · · ·
> DUCHESS. Will you hear me?
>   I'll never marry:—
> CARDINAL. So most widows say:
>   But commonly that motion lasts no longer
>   Than the turning of an hour-glass—the funeral sermon
>   And it, end both together.
>
>   (1.1.293–304)

A handful of speeches later the sexual innuendo comes to a climax, and the Duchess reveals the accuracy of her brothers' predictions (confirming their dark travesty of female lasciviousness and "doubleness") simultaneously:

> FERDINAND. You are my sister—
>   This was my father's poinard: do you see?
>   I'd be loth to see 't rusty, 'cause 'twas his:—
>   A visor and a mask are whispering-rooms
>   That were ne'er built for goodness: fare ye well:—
>   And women like that part which, like the lamprey
>   Hath ne'er a bone in't.
> DUCHESS. Fie sir!
> FERDINAND. Nay,
>   I mean the tongue: variety of courtship: . . .
>   What cannot a neat knave with a smooth tale
>   Make a woman believe? Farewell lusty widow. [*Exit.*]
> DUCHESS. Shall this move me? If all my royal kindred
>   Lay in my way unto this marriage,
>   I'd make them my low footsteps.   (1.1.330–43)

The picture of stereotyped female virtue painted in advance of her appearance by the Duchess's infatuated servant (and subsequent husband) Antonio cannot compensate for the impact of this initial encounter: "I'll case the picture up. . . . / All her particular worth grows to this sum: / She stains the time past, lights the time to come" (1.1.207–9). The Duchess's "luxuriousness" (lustfulness) drives her powerfully into secret marriage and flouting of her brothers' wishes, just as Gertrude's sexuality, in *Hamlet,* drives her into her dead husband's brother's bed. Lower in her sexual drive than "a beast that wants discourse of reason," the Duchess of Malfi steps out of the path of duty and marries for lust. Thereafter she remains heroically determined to follow through the consequences of her initial base action, until her resoluteness is gradually commuted into the splendour of resigned passive acceptance of inevitable downfall:

> FERDINAND. How doth our sister duchess bear herself
>   In her imprisonment?
> BOSOLA. Nobly; I'll describe her:
>   She's sad, as one long us'd to't; and she seems
>   Rather to welcome the end of misery
>   Than shun it;—a behaviour so noble
>   As gives a majesty to adversity;
>   You may discern the shape of loveliness
>   More perfect in her tears, than in her smiles.
>   (4.1.1–8)

"Majesty" in the female hero is here at its most reassuring and admirable when associated with patient suffering: Griselda, the Virgin Mary, Hecuba prostrate with grief. A "convincing" representation of the developing psychology of the female hero is apparently the transformation of lascivious waywardness into emblematic chaste resignation.

    The impulsive offer of love by a woman is most likely to be a sign of unreliableness and untrustworthiness, if the male characters are allowed to have the final say in "reading" that offer. When Beatrice-Joanna, in *The Changeling,* takes the decision to follow her sensual desire and marry Alsemero, disposing of her husband-to-be, she is already embarked on the course which will lead to her obsessive sexual involvement with De Flores:

> DE FLORES.   If a woman
>   Fly from one point, from him she makes a husband,
>   She spreads and mounts then like arithmetic,
>   One, ten, a hundred, a thousand, ten thousand,

> Proves in time sutler to an army royal. . . .
> Methinks I feel her in mine arms already,
> Her wanton fingers combing out this beard,
> And being pleased, praising this bad face.
> Hunger and pleasure, they'll commend sometimes
> Slovenly dishes, and feed heartily on 'em,
> Nay, which is stranger, refuse daintier for 'em.
>   (2.2.60–152)

If we miss this patriarchal assumption in the drama we are bound to be bemused by subsequent developments. In *Othello,* Desdemona has amply demonstrated her driving sensuality and female unreliability by marrying for love, without parental consent:

> Look to her, Moor, if thou hast eyes to see;
> She has deceiv'd her father, and may thee.
>   (1.3.292–93)

Such careful intrusions into the drama reminding the audience of the sensual strain in the central female character should, I think, alert us to the *guilt* which adheres to such characters. In the eyes of the Jacobean audience they are above all *culpable,* and their *strength*—the ways in which they direct the action, scheme and orchestrate, evade the consequences of their impulsive decisions, and ultimately face resolutely the final outcome—need to be seen in this context. Over the years critics have tended to attempt complicated exonerations of the female heroes of the Jacobean drama, to make them "innocent" of the sexual slur. We should take another look at the case.

The acknowledged source for Webster's *The Duchess of Malfi* is William Painter's *The Palace of Pleasure* (1566/67), an extremely popular compendium of lively tales of domestic and court life, drawn from the ancient and European traditions. The twenty-third "nouel" is entitled, "The Duchess of Malfi, the infortunate marriage of a Gentleman, called Antonio Bologna, with the Duchess of Malfi, and the pitifull death of them both." The moral message of this novella is unequivocal, from the opening paragraphs of the tale:

> Wherefore it behoueth the Noble, and such as haue charge of Common wealth, to liue an honest lyfe, and beare their port vpryght, that none haue cause to take ill example vpon dyscourse of their deedes and naughtie life. And aboue all, that modestie ought to be kept by women, whome as their race, Noble birth, authoritie and name, maketh them more famous, euen so their

vertue, honestie, chastitie, and continencie more praiseworthy. And behouefull it is, that like as they wishe to be honoured aboue all other, so their life do make them worthy of that honour, without disgracing their name by deede or woorde, or blemishing that brightnesse which may commende the same. I greatly feare that all the Princely factes, the exploits and conquests done by the *Babylonian* Queene *Semyramis,* neuer was recommended with such praise, as hir vice had shame in records by those which left remembrance of ancient acts. Thus I say, bicause a woman being as it were the Image of sweetnesse, curtesie and shamefastnesse, so soone as she steppeth out of the right tracte, and leaueth the smel of hir duetie and modestie, bisides the denigration of hir honor, thrusteth hir self into infinite troubles and causeth the ruine of such which should be honored and praised, if womens allurement solicited them not to follie.

The litany of conventional cautions against "dishonest" behaviour sets the tone of the story. "Woman being as it were the Image of sweetenesse, curtisie and shamefastnesse" has no alternative: any single act which does not square with this emblem of passive and dutiful behaviour condemns the individual as "fallen" from the pedestal. An entire glorious military career is blotted out when Semyramis seduces her son.

In the dramatic version of *The Duchess of Malfi,* active sexuality codes for female breach of decorum. In the moment of disobeying her brothers and remarrying (remarrying a social inferior, to emphasise that this is "lust" not "duty"), the Duchess of Malfi asserts her sexual self. In so doing she is metamorphosed from ideal mirror of virtue ("Let all sweet ladies break their flatt'ring glasses / And dress themselves in her" [1.1.203–4]) into lascivious whore. It is not simply that her brothers view her as such; the dominant strain in the subsequent representation of her *is* such. And we have to ask ourselves what it is about that knowing step she takes which is sufficient to rock the social system and warrant such ritualised condemnation. From the moment of her assertion of sexual independence, the Duchess moves with dignity but inexorably towards a ritual chastisement worthy of a flagrant breach of public order. Thereafter her strength lies in her fortitude in the face of a doom she has brought upon herself.

Yet the initial stand taken by the Duchess retains its dramatic power, despite the fact that success is apparently never a real possibility, the threat to patriarchal order never an actual one. I want now to suggest that there was an area of early modern social order in which *apparently,* although not actually, women had become frighteningly strong and independent, and one which maps plausibly on to the dominant preoccupations of the drama. This is the idea of property inheritance and Land Law.

The sixteenth century in England was a period of major and far-reaching change in inheritance practice. Unfortunately, these changes are masked from the student of literature by blanket references, whenever some comment on customary inheritance is called for, to a ubiquitous law of primogeniture (inheritance of the entire estate by the eldest male heir). Immediately he has introduced his bastard son, Edmund, to Kent, in *King Lear,* Gloucester specifies his family position:

> But I have a son, sir, by order of law, some year elder than this, who yet is no dearer in my account: though this knave came something saucily to the world before he was sent for, yet was his mother fair.
>
> (1.1.17–20)

This we are told is to establish that Edgar is Gloucester's legitimate *heir* as well as his legitimate son, since either way he is *older* than Edmund. Lear himself, meanwhile, divides his kingdom by "partible" inheritance (equal division) among his daughters, in the absence of a male heir. Certainly by the sixteenth century this was considered to be the ideal state of affairs, as codified in English Land Law, but as recent historians and historians of the Land Law themselves are quick to point out, inheritance *practice* never conformed with the ideal, and consisted in modifying and evading the most stringent requirements of lineal inheritance as codified, because of disastrous consequences this could in practice have in fragmenting individual estates.

During the sixteenth and seventeenth centuries, great landowners, under direct threat from wealthy status-seeking burghers, tinkered energetically with legislation and precedent in a determined effort to keep their dwindling estates together. The issue, inevitably, came down to a head-on conflict between land (the nobleman's asset) and cash (the increasingly powerful asset of the expanding mercantile class). And at the heart of every "tinkering" to be found in the meticulously drawn up wills of the nobility and gentry of the period, one is almost certain to find a woman.

Even before demographic accident had produced a dangerous shortfall in male heirs, female kin had come to be seen as destructive of estate conservation. A daughter had to be provided with a dowry, part at least of which, in noble households, would be in the form of land. As soon as she produced an heir to her husband's line, that land became part of the alien line's permanent holdings (in the absence of an heir it would revert to her own family, either upon her death, or upon that of her husband). In the absence of any sons at all, the estate would be divided among the daughters—once again a catastrophe in terms of consolidation of power in the form of an intact estate. And finally, in the event of a nobleman's dying before his wife, one-third of all his lands passed not to his male heir, but to his dowager widow, for her use during her lifetime. This both imposed a considerable burden on the heir, and might, if she remarried, result once again in the partition of previously intact estates. One wonders whether the regular confusion of "dowry" and "dower" (entirely distinct in law) in popular parlance stemmed from the threat both represented to the continuity of male inheritance.

In their concern over the absence of male heirs, and over the damage being done to their estates by strict settlement and traditional patterns of inheritance, heads of household increasingly turned their attention to the settlements on daughters and on younger sons. Traditionally these had taken the form of "portions" allocated in place of land at the time when the younger children left home. Increasingly landowners concentrated on these settlements to compensate for the erosion of the main estates: if a well-dowried girl could attract a good husband, or a younger son make a match with a wealthy heiress or widow on the strength of his portion, that might compensate for the initial outlay. Particularly important for the bargaining power of dowries was the fact that the daughter's dowry in goods was available to the *father* of the bridegroom to pay his debts in ready money (lands could not be easily "alienated"—sold out of the inheritance pattern).

Portions for younger sons and marriageable daughters increase dramatically during the Elizabethan and Jacobean periods. "Dowry inflation" was considered the curse of the age, decried by clergy and lawyers:

> The excesses of our times in giving great Dowries is growen to such a height, that it impoverisheth oftentimes the Parents; it seemeth a point worthy the consideration whether it were not expedient that the Parliament should limit the quantity of Dowries according to the State and Condition of every Man; which no doubt would greatly ease the Nobility and Gentry.

The effectiveness of the strategy as a lure is evidenced by the fact that some sumptuary legislation (legislation controlling richness of dress according to rank and status) aligned the permitted richness of dress for a woman with the size of her marriage portion. In Thomas Heywood's *A Woman Killed with Kindness,* the shifting fortunes of Mountford are directly reflected on stage by the dress his sister wears, and this in turn decides her desirability as a bride:

> Enter SIR CHARLES, *gentlemanlike, and his Sister, gentlewomanlike.*
> SUSAN. Brother, why have you trick'd me like a bride?
>   Bought me this gay attire, these ornaments?
>   Forget you our estate, our poverty.

(scene 14)

The woman's dress defines her power as a magnet to attract wealth on behalf of the paternal line.

The prominent position occupied by female heirs in all this discussion of the complex tactical manoeuvres surrounding inheritance is in striking contrast to their enforced submissiveness elsewhere within the Elizabethan and Jacobean social systems. This fact is, of course, somewhat ironic. It was not the intention of lawyers and landowners preoccupied with patrilinear succession to involve their women as other than means to a patriarchal end. But it remains true that female nobles and gentry do obtrude during this period in their capacity as carriers of inheritance.

Not that this gave them any *actual* power, and this is really the point at issue. They are technically strong (or strong enough to cause patriarchal anxiety), but actually in thrall. In Middleton's *Women Beware Women,* the handsomely dowried Isabella bewails her lack of personal choice of a marriage partner whilst at the same time affirming her importance in the inheritance stakes:

> ISABELLA.   Oh the heart breakings
>   Of miserable maids, where love's enforced!
>   The best condition is but bad enough:
>   When women have their choices, commonly
>   They do but buy their thraldoms, and bring great
>   portions
>   To men to keep 'em in subjection—
>   As if a fearful prisoner should bribe
>   The keeper to be good to him, yet lies in still,
>   And glad of a good usage, a good look sometimes.
>   By 'r Lady, no misery surmounts a woman's:
>   Men buy their slaves, but women buy their masters.

(1.2.166–76)

Yet in *Women Beware Women* it is in fact the female characters who, while formally protesting their ineffectualness, weakness and submissiveness to men, wheel-and-deal their way through adultery, murder and incest. The alliance of the heart which Isabella would prefer to an arranged marriage with a wealthy ward is an incestuous relationship with her uncle: the female drive towards independent choice leads to sexual licence. The shift from passivity to bravura activity is accompanied by a marked moral decline, apparent in her subsequent disparaging remarks on the indignity of being "marketed" as an heiress:

> ISABELLA. (*aside*) But that I have th'advantage of the fool,
> As much as woman's heart can wish and joy at,
> What an infernal torment 'twere to be
> Thus bought and sold, and turned and pried into:
> when alas
> The worst bit is too good for him! And the comfort is
> 'Has but a cater's place on't, and provides
> All for another's table.
>
> (3.4.33–39)

With comparable bravado, the Duchess of Malfi resolutely identifies her elevated fiscal position (as a young widow to a large estate, and heiress in her own right) with her actual entitlement to act exactly as she chooses:

> DUCHESS. The misery of us that are born great—
> We are forc'd to woo, because none dare woo us:
>
> . . . .
>
> sir, be confident—
> What is't distracts you? This is flesh, and blood, sir;
> 'Tis not the figure cut in alabaster
> Kneels at my husband's tomb. Awake, awake, man!
> I do here put off all vain ceremony,
> And only do appear to you a young widow
> That claims you for her husband, and like a widow,
> I use but half a blush in't.
>
> (1.1.441–59)

In both cases, I suggest, we are witness to the acting out of a taboo. As the loyal Cariola comments on the Duchess's behaviour:

> Whether the spirit of greatness or of woman
> Reign most in her, I know not, but it shows
> A fearful madness.
>
> (1.1.504–6)

The Duchess acts out her remarriage and its consequences *as if* her force-fulness as royal heir, dowager of the Dukedom of Amalfi, carrier of a substantial dowry in movable goods (which she and Antonio take legitimately with them when they flee together), gave her *real* power. In this she is proved pathetically wrong. In a passage which modern producers prefer to omit as tedious, the patriarchy's retaliation for her behaviour is spelt out:

> 2ND PILGRIM.   They are banish'd.
> 1ST PILGRIM. But I would ask what power hath this state
>   Of Ancona to determine of a free prince?
> 2ND PILGRIM. They are a free state sir, and her brother show'd
>   How that the Pope, fore-hearing of her looseness,
>   Hath seiz'd into th' protection of the church
>   The dukedom, which she held as a dowager.
>
> (3.4.27–33)

The Duchess has lost her princely immunity through forfeiture of her dower—the forfeiture being because she has proved herself "loose" by marrying, without her brothers' consent, "so mean a person" as Antonio (who himself has his own lands confiscated for his "felony"). From this moment she is not, despite her own protests to the contrary, "Duchess of Malfi still":

> DUCHESS. Am I not thy duchess?
> BOSOLA. Thou art some great woman, sure, for riot
>   begins to sit on thy forehead, clad in gray hairs,
>   twenty years sooner than on a merry milkmaid's.
>   Thou sleepest worse than if a mouse should be forced to
>   take up her lodging in a cat's ear: a little infant that
>   breeds its teeth, should it lie with thee, would cry out, as
>   if thou were the more unquiet bedfellow.
> DUCHESS. I am Duchess of Malfi still.
> BOSOLA. That makes thy sleep so broken.
>
> (4.2.134–43)

Proved pathetically wrong in her belief in emancipation through hereditary strength, the Duchess is reduced to the safe composite stereotype of penitent whore, Virgin majestic in grief, serving mother, and patient and true turtle dove mourning her one love. The Duchess acts out on stage her inheritance power which in real life was no power at all for the individual woman. In real life the verdict was decided upon in advance. As Painter put it:

> Behold here (O ye foolish louers) a Glasse of your lightnesse, and ye women, the course of your fonde behauior . . . Shall I be of opinion that a houshold seruaunt ought to sollicite, nay rather suborne the daughter of his Lord without punishment, or that a vile and abiect person dare to mount vpon a Princes bed? No no, pollicie requireth order in all, and eche wight ought to be matched according to their qualitie, without making a pastime of it to couer our follies, and know not of what force loue and desteny be, except the same be resisted. A goodly thing it is to loue, but where reason loseth his place, loue is without his effect, and the sequele rage and madnesse.

In Webster's play, the spectre of real female strength implicit in the inheritance structure is ritually exorcised. Headstrong, emancipated female love is chastened into figurative submission.

The general lesson to be learned from all this is, I hope, clear. Whatever is to be discovered by considering women figures in literature, it is unlikely to be a simple matter to read it out of the text of novel or play. However much of an inspiration the Duchess may appear to us—the strong woman challenging conventional attitudes—she is not a "real" woman, neither is she a direct reflection of individual women of her time. She is a transposition of a complex of attitudes towards women into a "travesty" (literally, a man in woman's clothes) of seventeenth-century womanhood. The strength we enjoy in performance is her actual weakness—perhaps that is what makes the Duchess of Malfi so captivating and poignant a stage figure.

Chronology

ca. 1580	John Webster born, place unknown.
ca. 1598	Admitted to the Middle Temple.
1602	Collaborates on various plays, including *Caesar's Fall* (lost) with Munday, Drayton, Middleton, and *Lady Jane* with Chettle, Dekker, Heywood, Smith.
1604	Webster and Dekker collaborate on *Westward Ho!* and *Northward Ho!*. Webster writes the induction for Marston's *Malcontent* and verses for Stephen Harrison's *Arches of Triumph*.
1607	Dekker and Webster publish *The Famous Historie of Sir Thomas Wyatt*.
ca. 1611	*The White Devil* published. Webster contributes verses to Heywood's *An Apology for Actors*.
1613	*The Duchess of Malfi* played by the King's Men at Blackfriars Theatre.
1615	Webster edits the third edition of Overbury's *Characters*.
1617	Revises *The Duchess of Malfi* for a stage revival.
1619	*The Devil's Law-Case* produced.
1624	Webster collaborates with Dekker, Ford, and Rowley on *Keep the Widow Waking* (lost); publishes *Monuments of Honour,* a pageant; collaborates with Rowley on *A Cure for a Cuckold*.
ca. 1634	Webster dies.

Contributors

HAROLD BLOOM, Sterling Professor of the Humanities at Yale University, is the author of *The Anxiety of Influence, Poetry and Repression,* and many other volumes of literary criticism. His forthcoming study, *Freud: Transference and Authority,* attempts a full-scale reading of all of Freud's major writings. A MacArthur Prize Fellow, he is the general editor of five series of literary criticism published by Chelsea House. During 1987–88, he was appointed Charles Eliot Norton Professor of Poetry at Harvard University.

MICHAEL R. BEST is Professor of English at the University of Victoria, British Columbia. He is the author of several articles on John Lyly and is coeditor of *The Book of Secrets of Albertus Magnus.*

LESLIE DUER is Associate Professor of English at McGill University.

M. C. BRADBROOK was Lecturer in English at Cambridge University. She is the author of *Themes and Conventions of Elizabethan Tragedy* and *The Growth and Structure of Elizabethan Comedy.*

BETTIE ANNE DOEBLER is Professor of English at Arizona State University. She is the author of *The Quickening Seed: Death in the Sermons of John Donne.*

JACQUELINE PEARSON is Lecturer in English Literature at the Victoria University of Manchester. She has written on the role of women in the Renaissance.

JOHN L. SELZER is Professor of English at Pennsylvania State University. His most recent publication is a study of Faulkner.

CATHERINE BELSEY is Lecturer in English at University College, Cardiff, Wales. She is the author of *Critical Practice* and *The Subject of Tragedy: Identity and Difference in Renaissance Drama.*

LISA JARDINE is Lecturer in English at Cambridge University. She is the author of *Francis Bacon: Discovery and the Art of Discourse* and *Still Harping on Daughters: Women and Drama in the Age of Shakespeare.*

131

Bibliography

Allison, Alexander W. "Ethical Themes in *The Duchess of Malfi.*" *Studies in English Literature 1500–1900* 4 (1964): 263–74.

Ausaire, K. H. *John Webster: Image, Patterns and Canon.* Jullunder City, India: Jalaluddin Rumi, 1969.

Baker, Susan C. "The Static Protagonist in *The Duchess of Malfi.*" *Texas Studies in Literature and Language* 22 (1980): 343–57.

Bawcutt, N. W. "*Don Quixote,* Part 1, and *The Duchess of Malfi.*" *The Modern Language Review* 66 (1971): 488–91.

Bergeron, David. "The Wax Figures in *The Duchess of Malfi.*" *Studies in English Literature 1500–1900* 18 (1978): 331–39.

Berlin, Normand. "*The Duchess of Malfi:* Act 5." *Genre* 3 (1970): 351–63.

Berry, Ralph. *The Art of John Webster.* Oxford: Clarendon, 1972.

Bliss, Lee. *The Word's Perspective: John Webster and the Jacobean Drama.* New Brunswick, N.J.: Rutgers University Press, 1983.

Bogard, Travis. *The Tragic Satire of John Webster.* Berkeley and Los Angeles: University of California Press, 1955.

Boklund, Gunnar. The Duchess of Malfi: *Sources, Themes, Characters.* Cambridge: Harvard University Press, 1962.

Boyer, C. V. *The Villain as Hero in Elizabethan Tragedy.* London: George Routledge; New York: Dutton, 1914.

Bradbrook, M. C. *English Dramatic Form.* New York: Barnes & Noble, 1965.

———. *Themes and Conventions of Elizabethan Tragedy.* Cambridge: Cambridge University Press, 1969.

———. "Two Notes upon Webster." *Modern Language Review* 42 (1947): 287–94.

Brennan, Elizabeth. "The Relationship between Brother and Sister in the Plays of John Webster." *Modern Language Review* 58 (1963): 488–94.

Brooke, Rupert. *John Webster and the Elizabethan Drama.* London: Sidgwick & Jackson, 1916.

Calderwood, James L. "*The Duchess of Malfi:* Styles of Ceremony." *Essays in Criticism* 12 (1963): 133–47.

Davies, C. W. "The Structure of *The Duchess of Malfi:* An Approach." *English* 12 (1958): 83–93.

Dent, R. W. *John Webster's Borrowing.* Berkeley and Los Angles: University of California Press, 1960.

Driscoll, James P. "Integrity of Life in *The Duchess of Malfi*." *Drama Survey* 6 (1967): 42–53.

Ekeblad, Inga-Stina. "The 'Impure Art' of John Webster." *The Review of English Studies* 9 (1958): 253–67.

———. "A Webster Villain: A Study of Character Imagery in *The Duchess of Malfi*." *Orpheus* 3 (1956): 126–33.

Ellis-Fermor, Una. *The Jacobean Drama*. London: Methuen, 1936.

Empson, William. " 'Mine Eyes Dazzle.' " *Essays in Criticism* 14 (1964): 80–86.

Emslie, McD. "Motives in Malfi." *Essays in Criticism* 9 (1959): 391–405.

Forker, Charles R. "Love, Death and Fame: The Grotesque Tragedy of John Webster." *Anglia* 91 (1973): 194–218.

———. "The Love-Death Nexus in English Renaissance Tragedy." *Shakespeare Survey* 8 (1975): 211–30.

Gianetti, Louis D. "A Contemporary View of *The Duchess of Malfi*." *Comparative Drama* 3 (1969-70): 297–307.

Goreau, Eloise. *Integrity of Life: Allegorical Imagery in the Plays of John Webster*. Salzburg: Institut für Englische Sprache und Literatur, 1974.

Hawkins, Harriet. " 'The Victim's Side': Webster's *Duchess of Malfi* and Chaucer's *Canterbury Tales*." In *Poetic Freedom and Poetic Truth*. London: Clarendon Press, 1976.

Hunter, G. K. and S. K., eds. *John Webster: A Critical Anthology*. Harmondsworth: Penguin, 1969.

Jack, Ian. "The Case of John Webster." *Scrutiny* 16 (1959): 38–53.

Jardine, Lisa. *Still Harping on Daughters: Women and Drama in the Age of Shakespeare*. Totowa, N.J.: Barnes & Noble, 1983.

Langman, F. H. "Truth and Effect in *The Duchess of Malfi*." *Sydney Studies in English* 6 (1980–81): 30–48.

Leech, Clifford. *Webster:* The Duchess of Malfi. Great Neck, New York: Barron's Educational Series, Inc., 1963.

———. *John Webster: A Critical Study*. London: The Hogarth Press, 1951.

Lord, Joan M. "*The Duchess of Malfi:* 'the Spirit of Greatness' and 'of Woman.' " *Studies in English Literature 1500–1900* 16 (Spring 1976): 305–17.

Luecke, Jame Marie. "*The Duchess of Malfi:* Comic and Satiric Confusion in a Tragedy." *Studies in English Literature 1500–1900* 4 (1964): 275–90.

Moore, Don D. *John Webster and His Critics, 1617–1964*. Baton Rouge: Louisiana State University Press, 1966.

Morris, Brian, ed. *John Webster: Critical Commentaries*. London: Ernest Benn, 1970.

Mulryne, J. R. " 'The White Devil' and 'The Duchess of Malfi.' " In *Jacobean Theatre,* Stratford-Upon-Avon Studies, vol. 1, 201–26. London: E. Arnold, 1960.

Murray, Peter B. *A Study of John Webster*. The Hague: Mouton, 1969.

Neill, Michael. "Monuments and Ruins as Symbols in *The Duchess of Malfi*." In *Drama and Symbolism,* edited by James Redmond. Cambridge: Cambridge University Press, 1982.

Ornstein, Robert. *The Moral Vision of Jacobean Tragedy*. Madison: University of Wisconsin Press, 1960.

Peterson, Joyce E. *Curs'd Example:* The Duchess of Malfi and *Commonwealth Tragedy*. Columbia: University of Missouri Press, 1978.

Praz, Mario. "John Webster and *The Maid's Tragedy*." *English Studies* 37 (1956): 252–58.

Price, Hereward T. "The Function of Imagery in Webster." *PMLA* 70 (1955): 717–39.

Prior, Moody E. *The Language of Tragedy*. New York: Columbia University Press, 1947.

Rabkin, Norman, ed. *Twentieth Century Interpretations of* The Duchess of Malfi: *A Collection of Critical Essays*. Englewood Cliffs, N.J.: Prentice-Hall, 1968.

Ribner, Irving. *Jacobean Tragedy: The Quest for Moral Order*. 1962. Reprint. Totowa, N.J.: Rowman, 1979.

Riewald, J. G. "Shakespeare Burlesque in John Webster's *The Duchess of Malfi*." In *English Studies Presented to R. W. Zandvoort*, 177–89. Amsterdam: Swets & Zeitlinger, 1964.

Schuman, Samuel. "The Ring and the Jewel in Webster's Tragedies." *Texas Studies in Literature and Language* 14 (1972): 253–68.

Stoll, E. E. *John Webster: The Periods of His Work as Determined by His Relations to the Drama of His Day*. Boston: A. Mudge & Son, 1905.

Thayer, C. G. "The Ambiguity of Bosola." *Studies in Philology* 54 (1957): 162–71.

Tillyard, E. M. W. *The Elizabethan World Picture*. 1943. Reprint. London: Chatto & Windus, 1967.

Vernon, P. F. "The Duchess of Malfi's Guilt." *Notes and Queries* n.s. 10 (1963): 335–38.

Wadsworth, Frank W. "Webster's *Duchess of Malfi* in the Light of Some Contemporary Ideas on Marriage and Remarriage." *Philological Quarterly* 35 (1956): 394–407.

Whitman, Robert F. "The Moral Paradox of Webster's Tragedy." *PMLA* 90 (1975): 894–903.

Wilkinson, Charles. "Twin Structures in John Webster's *The Duchess of Malfi*." *Literature and Psychology* 31 (1981): 52–65.

Acknowledgments

"A Precarious Balance: Structure in *The Duchess of Malfi*" by Michael R. Best from *Shakespeare and Some Others: Essays on Shakespeare and Some of his Contemporaries,* edited by Alan Brissenden, © 1976 by Michael R. Best. Reprinted by permission.

"The Landscape of Imagination in *The Duchess of Malfi*" by Leslie Duer from *Modern Language Studies* 10, no. 1 (Winter 1979–80), © 1980 by the Northeast Modern Language Association. Reprinted by permission.

"Renaissance Contexts for *The Duchess of Malfi*" (originally entitled *"The Duchess of Malfi"*) by M. C. Bradbrook from *John Webster: Citizen and Dramatist* by M. C. Bradbrook, © 1980 by M. C. Bradbrook and Weidenfeld & Nicolson, Ltd., London. Reprinted by permission of the author and Columbia University Press.

"Continuity in the Art of Dying: *The Duchess of Malfi*" by Bettie Anne Doebler from *Comparative Drama* 14, no. 3 (Fall 1980), © 1980 by Clifford Davidson, C. J. Gianakaris, and John H. Stroupe. Reprinted by permission of the editors of *Comparative Drama.*

" 'To Behold my Tragedy': Tragedy and Anti-tragedy in *The Duchess of Malfi*" by Jacqueline Pearson from *Tragedy and Tragicomedy in the Plays of John Webster* by Jacqueline Pearson, © 1980 by Jacqueline Pearson. Reprinted by permission of Barnes & Noble Books, Totowa, New Jersey and Manchester University Press.

"Merit and Degree in Webster's *The Duchess of Malfi*" by John L. Selzer from *English Literary Renaissance* 11, no. 1 (Winter 1981), © 1981 by *English Literary Renaissance.* Reprinted by permission of the editors of *English Literary Renaissance.*

"Emblem and Antithesis in *The Duchess of Malfi*" by Catherine Belsey from *Renaissance Drama* n.s. 11 (1981), © 1981 by Northwestern University Press. Reprinted by permission of Northwestern University Press.

"*The Duchess of Malfi:* A Case Study in the Literary Representation of Women" by Lisa Jardine from *Teaching the Text,* edited by Suzanne Kappeler and Norman Bryson, © 1983 by Lisa Jardine. Reprinted by permission of Routledge & Kegan Paul Ltd.

Index